CliffsNotes™

Using Your First iMac™

by Jennifer Watson

IN THIS BOOK

- Install your new iMac
- Connect to the Internet
- Write letters and draw pictures
- Keep your iMac running smoothly
- Reinforce what you learn with CliffsNotes Review
- Find more iMac information in CliffsNotes Resource Center and online at www.cliffsnotes.com

IDG Books Worldwide, Inc.
An International Data Group Company
Foster City, CA • Chicago, IL • Indianapolis, IN • New York, NY

About the Author

Jennifer Watson is the author of *Teach Yourself the iMac* and ten other popular and bestselling books on computers and the Internet.

Publisher's Acknowledgments

Editorial

Senior Project Editor: Pat O'Brien
Acquisitions Editor: Steven H. Hayes
Copy Editor: Ted Cains
Technical Editor: Marita Ellixson, Phil Robertson
Editorial Assistant: Jamila Pree

Production

Indexer: York Production Services
Proofreader: York Production Services
IDG Books Indianapolis Production Department

CliffsNotes™ Using Your First iMac™
Published by
IDG Books Worldwide, Inc.
An International Data Group Company
919 E. Hillsdale Blvd.
Suite 400
Foster City, CA 94404
www.idgbooks.com (IDG Books Worldwide Web site)
www.cliffsnotes.com (CliffsNotes Web site)

Library of Congress Catalog Card No.: 99-64203
ISBN: 0-7645-8527-4
Printed in the United States of America
10 9 8 7 6 5 4 3 2 1
1O/SU/QY/ZZ/IN
Distributed in the United States by IDG Books Worldwide, Inc.
Distributed by CDG Books Canada Inc. for Canada; by Transworld Publishers Limited in the United Kingdom; by IDG Norge Books for Norway; by IDG Sweden Books for Sweden; by IDG Books Australia Publishing Corporation Pty. Ltd. for Australia and New Zealand; by TransQuest Publishers Pte Ltd. for Singapore, Malaysia, Thailand, Indonesia, and Hong Kong; by Gotop Information Inc. for Taiwan; by ICG Muse, Inc. for Japan; by Norma Comunicaciones S.A. for Colombia; by Intersoft for South Africa; by Eyrolles for France; by International Thomson Publishing for Germany, Austria and Switzerland; by Distribuidora Cuspide for Argentina; by LR International for Brazil; by Galileo Libros for Chile; by Ediciones ZETA S.C.R. Ltda. for Peru; by WS Computer Publishing Corporation, Inc., for the Philippines; by Contemporanea de Ediciones for Venezuela; by Express Computer Distributors for the Caribbean and West Indies; by Micronesia Media Distributor, Inc. for Micronesia; by Grupo Editorial Norma S.A. for Guatemala; by Chips Computadoras S.A. de C.V. for Mexico; by Editorial Norma de Panama S.A. for Panama; by American Bookshops for Finland. Authorized Sales Agent: Anthony Rudkin Associates for the Middle East and North Africa.
For general information on IDG Books Worldwide's books in the U.S., please call our Consumer Customer Service department at **800-762-2974**. For reseller information, including discounts and premium sales, please call our Reseller Customer Service department at **800-434-3422**.
For information on where to purchase IDG Books Worldwide's books outside the U.S., please contact our International Sales department at 317-596-5530 or fax **317-596-5692**.
For consumer information on foreign language translations, please contact our Customer Service department at **1-800-434-3422**, fax **317-596-5692**, or e-mail rights@idgbooks.com.
For information on licensing foreign or domestic rights, please phone **+1-650-655-3109**.
For sales inquiries and special prices for bulk quantities, please contact our Sales department at 650-655-3200 or write to the address above.
For information on using IDG Books Worldwide's books in the classroom or for ordering examination copies, please contact our Educational Sales department at **800-434-2086** or fax **317-596-5499**.
For press review copies, author interviews, or other publicity information, please contact our Public Relations department at **650-655-3000** or fax **650-655-3299**.
For authorization to photocopy items for corporate, personal, or educational use, please contact Copyright Clearance Center, 222 Rosewood Drive, Danvers, MA 01923, or fax **978-750-4470**.

Table of Contents

INTRODUCTION

Bringing home an iMac is the start of a fun, productive relationship. This book is designed to make that relationship even less stressful.

Why Do You Need This Book?

Can you answer yes to any of these questions?

- Do you need to learn about the iMac fast?
- Don't have time to read 500 pages about your new computer?
- Want to access the Internet in record time?
- Itching to write a letter to Mom?

If so, then CliffsNotes *Using Your First iMac* is for you!

How to Use This Book

You're the boss here. You get to decide how to use this book. You can either read the book from cover to cover or just look for the information you want and put it back on the shelf for later. However, I'll tell you about a few ways I recommend to search for your topics.

- Use the index in the back of the book.
- Flip through the book looking for your topic in the running heads.
- Look in the table of contents in the front of the book.
- Look at the In This Chapter list at the beginning of each chapter.
- Look for additional information in the Resource Center or test your knowledge in the Review section.

Also, to find important information quickly, you can look for *icons* strategically placed in the text. Here is a description of the icons you'll find in this book:

If you see a Remember icon, make a mental note of this text — it's worth keeping in mind.

If you see a Tip icon, you'll know you've run across a helpful hint, uncovered a secret, or received good advice.

The Warning icon alerts you to something that could be dangerous, requires special caution, or should be avoided.

Don't Miss Our Web Site

Keep up with the exciting world of computing by visiting the CliffsNotes Web site at `www.cliffsnotes.com`. Here's what you find:

- Interactive tools that are fun and informative
- Links to interesting Web sites
- Additional resources to help you continue your learning

At `www.cliffsnotes.com`, you can even register for a new feature called CliffsNotes Daily, which offers you newsletters on a variety of topics, delivered right to your e-mail inbox each business day.

If you haven't yet discovered the Internet and are wondering how to get online, pick up *Getting On the Internet*, new from CliffsNotes. You learn just what you need to make your online connection quickly and easily. See you at `www.cliffsnotes.com`!

CHAPTER 1

STARTING FAST

IN THIS CHAPTER

- Identifying the parts
- Setting up
- Powering up
- Using the mouse and keyboard
- Using the Mac OS Setup Assistant
- Shutting down

If this is your very first Macintosh computer, come along with me to find out how to unpack your iMac and set it up so that it works best for you. I also show you how to turn it on, use those funky things called a mouse and a keyboard, make some basic settings, and then shut it down. Along the way, you master some basic Mac skills, such as clicking, selecting, and more.

If this isn't your first Mac, just skim this chapter. The information on identifying the iMac's parts and setting up the iMac should be valuable.

Identifying the Parts

The first thing you want to do when you get your iMac is identify the parts. If your iMac is still in its box, start by moving the box to a wide open area with good lighting. I recommend placing the box on the floor. Carefully open the box and remove the Accessory Kit or the top. Your iMac Accessory Kit should contain the following:

- Documentation
- CD-ROM folio
- Two cables
- Mouse
- Keyboard

If you're not sure what these things look like, I describe them in a moment.

Now remove the packing material and peer inside the box again. You should see your new iMac snuggled in the box. If you ordered anything along with your iMac (a book, a CD, and so on), you may find it in a separate box.

Leave your iMac in the box for now and turn your attention back to the Accessory Kit. The documentation sent with your iMac consists of a few simple brochures that explain how to set up your iMac and how to get more help. You also see some software-related documentation. I recommend you read all this documentation at some point; right now, locate the "Welcome to your iMac" card. It has bright, glossy photos depicting the iMac setup. Use this card to identify your iMac's components if you're not sure what they look like. Here a list of the components:

- The *power cord* (which may be colored to match your iMac) has a three-prong plug at one end and a three-prong receptacle at the other.
- The *telephone line cable* (which may be translucent) has standard plugs at each end.
- The *mouse* is round with an attached cable; it's colored to match your iMac.
- The *keyboard* has black keys, colored trim to match your iMac, and an attached cable.

Remove each component from the Accessory Kit and set them near where you plan to set up your iMac.

If any components are missing or your iMac isn't in the color you ordered, contact the store or dealer before you go any further. Otherwise, it's time to set up your iMac!

Setting Up

Before you ask how to set up your iMac, ask yourself *where* you want to set it up. Your kitchen table probably isn't the best place. Desks work better, preferably those with plenty of room for your iMac plus the keyboard and mouse. You also want plenty of elbow room and leg room, as well as task lamps that you can use to, say, read this book. Be sure an AC power outlet and a telephone jack are nearby, too.

After you have your iMac's new home picked out, lift the iMac out of the box using the handhold in the top of your iMac while supporting the bottom. Don't use the foot (the handle-like thing on the bottom of the iMac) as a handle — it's too fragile. Set the iMac down on your desk gently. You can flip down the foot to change the monitor's viewing angle.

Here's how to set up and connect all your iMac's components:

1. Turn your iMac a bit to the left so that you can open the access door on the right side.
2. Look farther beyond the access door, toward the rear of the iMac, for the recessed power socket.
3. Plug the receptacle end of the power cord into the socket, and then plug the other end into a three-prong wall outlet or a surge suppressor. If you use a surge suppressor (to guard against power surges that can damage your iMac), you want to plug the surge suppressor into the wall outlet.

4. Set your keyboard and mouse on the desk in front of your iMac.
5. Plug the end of the mouse cable into one of the sockets on the side of your keyboard (use the right side if you're right-handed).
6. Open the access door on the side of your iMac and find the two USB (Universal Serial Bus) sockets inside. You can identify the USB ports by matching the symbol on the end of your keyboard cable to the symbols on the ports — the symbol looks a bit like a pitchfork.
7. Plug the keyboard cable into either USB port.
8. If you intend to use the Internet, plug your telephone line cable into the modem jack (also behind the access door) and plug the other end of the telephone cable into a standard telephone wall jack.
9. Close the access door so that the cables snake out the two notches in the lower corners of the door (not the finger hole), and turn your iMac back so that it faces you.

That's it! Your iMac is ready to go.

Powering Up

The moment you've been waiting for has arrived: It's time to give your iMac life! Powering up the iMac is easy. Every iMac has a power button at the bottom right of the computer, below the screen. Newer iMacs also have a power button on the keyboard. Both power buttons are round and have a symbol that looks like a circle with a line through it. Push either one of these power buttons to turn on your iMac.

Upon pushing a power button, you hear the famous Mac musical startup chime, and the power button on the monitor (computer screen) turns orange and then green. Your iMac monitor turns on and welcomes you with a happy-faced Mac, followed by the Mac OS logo. (Mac OS, pronounced "mac oh es," is the name of the operating system that runs your iMac.) Along the bottom of your monitor, you should see a series of icons (small pictures) appear one after another in quick succession. After a minute (or less if you have a newer iMac), the startup process finishes and your iMac displays its desktop on the monitor.

The *desktop* (also called the *Finder*) is where you begin and end every session. It fills your screen with icons, windows, and a bunch of stuff that may seem strange if this is your first time using a Mac (see Figure 1-1). Don't worry if you don't recognize these terms yet — I explain them throughout the book.

Figure 1-1: The desktop is your home base on the iMac.

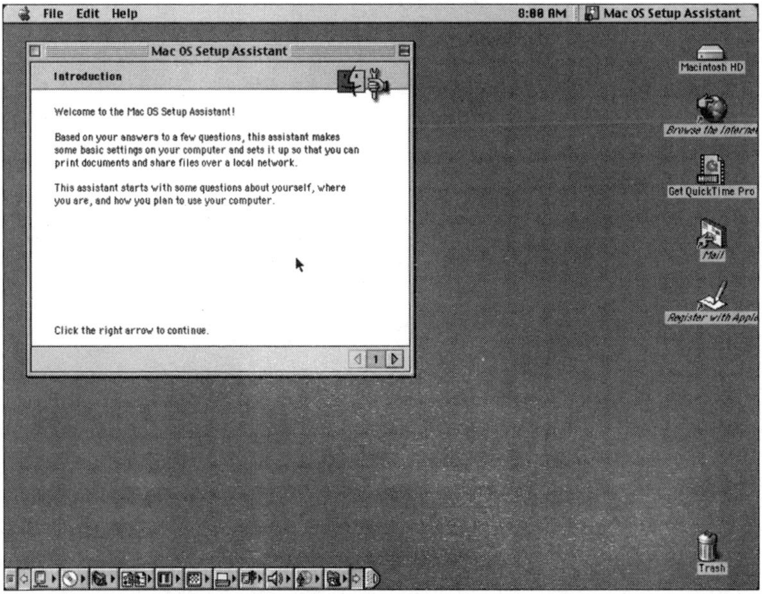

The first time you start up your iMac, the Mac OS Setup Assistant window opens and welcomes you. The Setup Assistant walks you through various settings for your iMac. For now, just ignore this window — I return to the Mac OS Setup Assistant at the end of this chapter.

Using the Mouse and Keyboard

The iMac mouse and keyboard look different, but they work like virtually any other mouse and keyboard. Already comfortable with how to use a mouse and keyboard? Feel free to skip ahead.

Getting a grip on your mouse

The iMac mouse, as cute as it is, can be a handful at first. To get the best grip on it, try these steps:

1. Place the mouse flat on the desk with the cord pointing away from you.
2. Place your index finger lightly on the large button near the cable end, between the Apple symbol and the cord (but don't depress the button).
3. Gently grasp the mouse with your thumb on one side and your remaining fingers on the other side. Feel free to rest your palm on the top of the desk.
4. Move the mouse freely around your desktop.

If you look closely at your mouse, you may see a ball moving around inside it as you move the mouse. Now look on your monitor for a small arrow mimicking the movement of the mouse. This arrow is your *pointer;* your mouse controls it. You use your pointer all the time on your iMac.

If you're new to computers in general, let me tell you about mouse pads. A *mouse pad* goes under your mouse to make the ball inside your mouse move more easily. You may find that the top of a desk or table is too slippery to get good traction for your mouse. I recommend going to a local computer store and getting yourself a mouse pad. You can choose from all sorts of designs; pick one that fits your interests.

You could just move the pointer around, but it doesn't do much by itself. You also need to *click* the button on the mouse by lightly pressing the button (you hear a "click") and then releasing it (another "click"). You hear just one click if you press and release faster. Try clicking your mouse in various places on your screen, such as on an *icon* (one of the little pictures on the desktop) or the *menu bar* (the white strip that runs across the top of the screen). Click only once (a *single-click*) at this point. You may also see single-clicking referred to as *selecting*. A selected item changes color (see Figure 1-2). You can *deselect* an item by clicking on an empty area of the iMac desktop.

Figure 1-2: The Macintosh HD icon in the upper-right corner is selected.

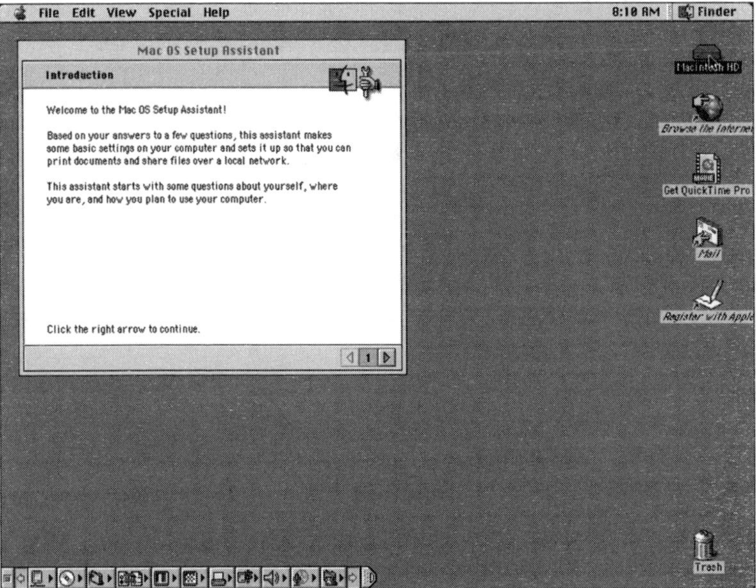

Typing on the keyboard

Now, turn your attention to the keyboard. To many first-time computer users, the keyboard can seem very daunting. Don't worry — you aren't expected to play your keyboard like a piano. The keyboard is a way to input information, like the buttons on a calculator.

You don't need to know what each key does right now, but it helps to understand a few. Here's another handy list for you:

- The keys in the middle with all the letters on them are mostly used to type words and sentences, and they work much like the keys on a typewriter.
- The Shift key also works the way it does on a typewriter — just hold down the Shift key and press a letter key to make a capital letter.
- The Caps Lock key turns all letters you type into capital letters, but it doesn't affect the numbers and punctuation marks — the Caps Lock key lights up when enabled.
- The Tab key also works much like a typewriter's tab key, shifting across the "page" in preset increments.
- Control, Option, and Command (the key with an Apple on it, which looks like this: ⌘) perform special operations and keyboard shortcuts when used in conjunction with other keys.
- The Space bar (the long bar without a name on it) inserts a blank space between words.
- The arrow keys in the lower-right corner move your insertion point up, down, left, and right.
- The Return key begins a new line of text when you need it, such as at the end of a paragraph.

- The Delete key "backspaces" over your text and erases it.
- The smaller group of keys on the right is the *number pad,* which performs much like a calculator.

You become intimately acquainted with each of these keys as you learn to use your iMac.

Mac OS Setup Assistant

The Mac OS Setup Assistant is not only a good way to set up the Mac OS, but a good exercise in using the mouse and keyboard, too. If you clicked around the screen while practicing your mouse skills, click once on the Mac OS Setup Assistant window to make it active. You notice that the window outline becomes darker when you do so. If you accidentally click outside the Mac OS Setup Assistant window during the setup process, just click on the window. Follow these steps to work your way through the Mac OS Setup Assistant:

1. Read the text in the Mac OS Setup Assistant window.
2. When you're ready, move your mouse so that the pointer is directly over the right arrow in the lower-right corner of the window. Now click once (press down and release quickly). You see the arrow button darken as you press down, and then the window changes immediately after you release. Should you want to go back to the previous window, click the left arrow, which is now available. (It was unavailable, or "grayed out," before.)
3. Choose the keyboard format settings you prefer. The choices appear in a *list box.* One of them ("U.S.") may already be selected for you — you can tell if it's selected by the darker or colored bar around the text. If your preference isn't U.S., or U.S. isn't selected, move your pointer to the format you prefer and click once to select it.

4. Click the right arrow again to continue. The Setup Assistant asks for your name and organization. Below the first question is a box into which you can type.
5. Move your pointer to the box, click once, and type your name.
6. Press the Tab key on your keyboard to jump to the second box.
7. Type your company, organization, or school name.
8. Click the right arrow key. The assistant asks you to verify the correct time and date. Below the first question are two buttons where you can reply "Yes" or "No." These buttons are called *radio buttons* because they work much like the old-fashioned push buttons on a radio — you can depress only one button at a time. To use a radio button, just move your pointer over the circle and click once — it either darkens (selected) or lightens (deselected).

   The next two questions have boxes like the previous window, only they have little arrow keys next to them. To use these boxes to answer the questions, click once on the number you wish to change and either type the new number on the keyboard or click the down or up arrow to adjust the numbers incrementally. You click each segment of the time or date to adjust it.
9. Click the right arrow to continue. This window asks you to choose the city that you live in or a city in the same time zone, so that your iMac can keep track of which time zone you live in. You have a list of options in a list box, much like the list box earlier. This time, however, the list is much longer. To see the entire list, use the arrows on the right side of the window to *scroll* through the list.
10. Click a city name to select it and continue on to the next window. When asked if you want to use a *Simple Finder,* I recommend that you answer No (make sure the No radio button is selected, or dark). The remaining windows ask

difficult questions that you may not be able to answer quite yet. You can continue clicking the right arrow button until you reach the last window, in which Mac OS Setup Assistant informs you that it's ready to make the basic settings.

11. Choose one of the options at the bottom of the window. You have three options:

    Show Details shows you each of the settings you just made — note that the Show Details button changes to Hide Details after you click it. If you see an error, you can use the left arrow button to go back to the appropriate window and fix it.

    Cancel enables you to stop the setup process. If you're not quite ready to finish the process, click Cancel; you can always come back to Mac OS Setup Assistant later.

    Go Ahead tells Mac OS Setup Assistant to set up your iMac according to the settings you input. After a few moments, the assistant announces that it completed its tasks successfully.

12. Click Quit to exit the Mac OS Setup Assistant.

Shutting Down

This chapter is almost over, but I can't leave you without showing you how to shut down your iMac. Don't worry — if you're still raring to go, you can skip this step and come back when you're ready to call it a day.

Your iMac offers a bunch of ways to shut down, or *power off.* The simplest way at this stage of the game is the power button on your keyboard (not the one on your iMac). If you have a power button on your keyboard, press it now. A small window, or a *dialog box,* pops up on your screen and asks you if you're sure you want to shut down your computer now (see Figure 1-3).

Figure 1-3: Which way do you go?

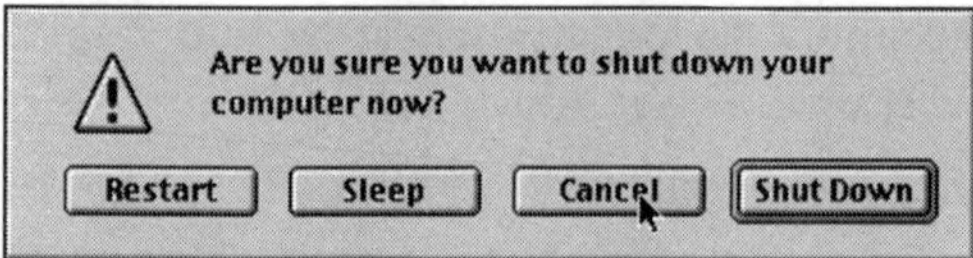

You have the following four options:

- **Restart** shuts down your iMac and then instantly restarts it for you. Use this after you install new software or when you just want a fresh start.
- **Sleep** puts your iMac in a low-power mode without actually shutting it down. You can wake up your iMac by pressing any key on the keyboard.
- **Cancel** aborts the shut down process completely so that you can return to using the iMac. Use this if you accidentally press the power button while the iMac is turned on.
- **Shut Down** powers down the iMac completely. You need to press the power button again to turn it back on later.

Another way to shut down your iMac is to move your pointer up to the word *Special* at the top of your screen. Click once on Special and a *menu* of options drops down. Move your pointer down the list to the Shut Down option at the bottom. Click once. Your iMac shuts down!

You can also shut down your iMac by pressing the power button on your iMac itself. Like the Shut Down option in the Special menu, your iMac shuts down immediately without asking you if you really want to shut down first. So press it only if you are truly ready to shut down.

Your iMac works best when you use its Shut Down feature. Don't switch off with your surge suppressor — it can lead to trouble later on.

CHAPTER 2

MASTERING YOUR DESKTOP

IN THIS CHAPTER

- Using menus
- Opening windows
- Identifying icons
- Finding files
- Using the Control Strip
- Changing preferences

Captain on the bridge! Well, almost. Your iMac desktop isn't too different from the bridge of a dazzling, high-tech ship — and you are its captain. On the desktop, you execute commands, make executive decisions, perform daily functions, and launch strategic missions into the depths of cyberspace. You think I'm kidding!

In all seriousness, the desktop *is* the command center of the iMac. Before you can give effective commands to your iMac, however, you need to understand how the controls themselves work.

Using Menus

Menus are everywhere on the iMac. You can order things from your iMac menus, or perhaps *giving* orders would be more accurate. Menus contain commands to do things like open files and shut down your iMac (as you saw in the last chapter). The desktop has several menus; all are available in the *menu bar* (the white bar with all the menu names) at the top of the screen.

The Apple menu

Starting from the left side, the first menu is the Apple menu (it looks like a multicolored apple). Click the Apple symbol once to pull down the menu. Items in the menu highlight as your pointer passes over them. When a menu item is highlighted, the item is selected. You can execute a selected command by clicking it once.

When you pass over a menu item with an arrow next to it, another menu appears. This second menu is called a *submenu;* you can select from it as well (see Figure 2-1).

Figure 2-1: The Apple menu has several submenus.

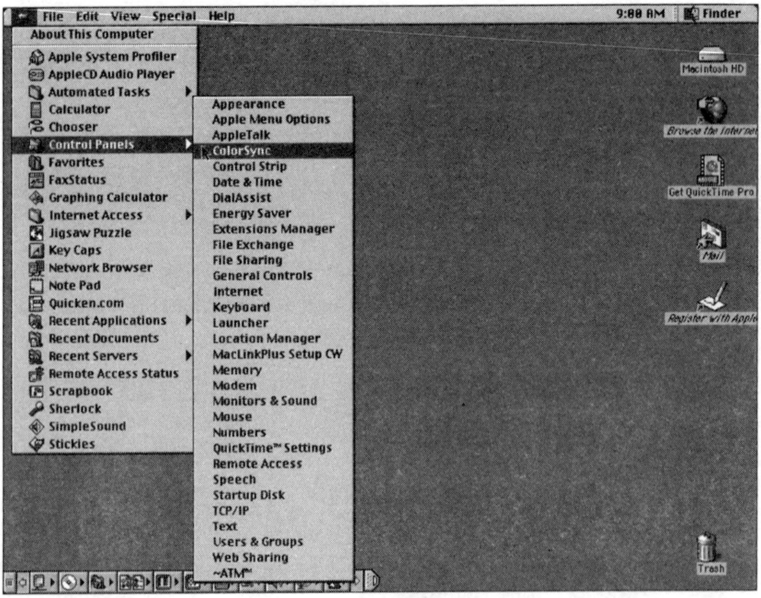

Another way to pull down a menu is to press and hold your mouse over a menu name in the menu bar. Keep pressing the mouse button as you move through the menu. When you see a menu item you like, make sure your pointer is over the menu item and then release your mouse button.

Before you begin executing commands, however, you may want to know what they actually do! The Apple menu has a bunch of *desk accessory* items, such as the Calculator and Note Pad. In many ways, your Apple menu is the equivalent of a circular organizer — it keeps important things within easy reach. The Apple menu is usually available no matter what you're doing on your iMac.

The File menu

To the right of the Apple menu is the File menu, which manipulates files on your desktop. Usually, you can open, print, save, and close your documents. You usually find a File menu throughout your iMac, though the options may differ depending on the program you're using.

The Edit menu

The Edit commands manipulate information and actions, such as Copy, Cut, Paste, and Select All. Your preferences for the desktop are located at the bottom of this menu; I tell you about desktop preferences later in this chapter. You almost always find an Edit menu on your iMac, though options may differ from program to program.

The View menu

The View menu offers commands to manipulate how items on the desktop look. You probably have your view set "as Icons" (the check mark in the menu indicates your setting) and thus you see items on your desktop as icons.

The Special menu

The Special menu commands perform the following disk- and computer-related functions:

- **Empty Trash** deletes files you placed in the Trash at the bottom of the screen.
- **Eject** spits out a CD-ROM or removable disk (if you have a peripheral to read them). You have to highlight the disk's icon on the desktop for this to work.
- **Erase Disk** permanently removes data from a disk (don't use this one yet).
- **Shut Down**, **Restart**, and **Sleep** work the same way as you learned at the end of the last chapter.

The Help menu

The Help menu offers the following commands that help you use your iMac:

- **Help Center** contains a collection of information about your iMac.
- **Show Balloons** displays helpful hints when your mouse pointer hovers over some items. This option changes to Hide Balloons when you activate it.
- **Tutorial** and **Mac OS Help** offer information on basic Mac skills.

Most programs also offer a Help menu.

The Application menu

The Application menu (the menu at the far right of your menu bar) switches between open programs. A check mark next to an item indicates the active program. If you don't have any programs currently open, only the Finder (desktop) is available. The Application menu is almost always available.

Opening Windows

Most of the commands in the menus open windows of one sort or another. A *window* is essentially a framed box that may contain options, information, questions, and so on. Most everything you see on your iMac will be in a window. Windows keep things organized.

The first window you saw when you powered up your iMac in Chapter 1 was the Mac OS Setup Assistant window. This window was for an *application,* or *software program*. If you'd like to take a better look at this window, go to your Apple menu, display the Recent Applications submenu, and choose Mac OS Setup Assistant. When the window appears on your desktop, notice the frame around it. The top bar with the stripes and the name of the window is called the *Title bar*. At one end of the Title bar is a plain box (the *Close box*) and at the other is a box with a line through it (the *Collapse box*). If you click the Collapse box, the window disappears and you see only the Title bar — this is useful when you want to make more room on your screen but don't want to close a window. If you click the Close box, you close the window completely.

Take a look at another window. Pull down your Apple menu, move your pointer down to the Control Panels option, and click once (ignore its submenu for now). A new window opens on your monitor and its Title bar identifies it as Control Panels (see Figure 2-2). If you look closely, you can see another box on the right side — this one has a smaller box inside of it. This is the *Zoom box*. Click it to enlarge the window. Click it again to return the window to its original size.

Figure 2-2: The Control Panels window.

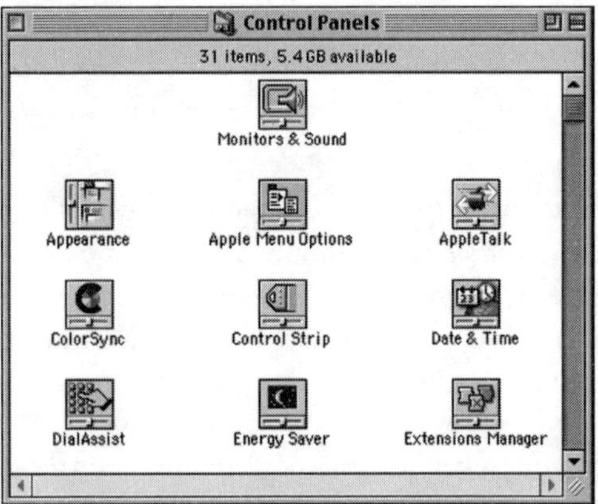

You may notice something else different about this new window. It has *scroll bars* on the right and bottom with arrows at the ends. An active scroll bar is gray with black arrows at each end and a small box within it, while an inactive scroll bar is simply white. To scroll up or down a window, single-click one of the arrows on your scroll bar. The small box in the scroll bar moves to show which section of the window's contents are displayed (the top or bottom, left or right, or somewhere in between). Your view of the window's contents changes accordingly. For precise or fast adjustments, follow these steps:

1. Place the tip of your pointer over the small box.
2. Click and hold down the mouse button.
3. Move the box to a new spot on the scroll bar. This process is called *dragging*. The window scrolls while you drag.
4. Release the mouse button when you find what you want. Another neat feature of this window is the ability to resize it. Look at the lower-right corner of the Control Panels window. Do you see the three diagonal lines? That's the Size box; simply click and drag this to resize your window to how you like it.

As you learn to use your iMac, you'll come across one other type of window: the *dialog box*. The "Are you sure you want to shut down your computer?" window that you saw at the end of Chapter 1 is a dialog box.

Note that you can't resize or collapse dialog boxes like you can other windows. You need to click one of its buttons to dismiss the window and continue.

Identifying Icons

Wondering about all those small pictures with words under them on the desktop and in your windows? These are *icons;* they represent various files on your iMac. Some also represent other windows, or *folders,* which contain files or even more folders. The Control Panels window you opened in the previous section is actually a folder with a bunch of files in it.

The first icon on your desktop (in the upper-right corner) is the Macintosh HD icon. (The "HD" stands for Hard Drive, which is where your iMac stores information electronically.) An icon's picture provides a visual clue to the kind of information it represents. This icon looks like a box — what your hard drive looks like inside your computer. Below the icon is the label ("Macintosh HD"). Most icons follow this format: small picture and label.

Icons are similar to menu items. As with menus, you can select and activate items represented by icons. You select an icon by positioning the tip of your pointer over it and clicking once. Your icon changes color (is highlighted) after you select it. To activate an icon, just double-click it — a *double-click* is two mouse clicks (down, up, down, up) in rapid succession. As with menu items, knowing what an icon does before you activate it is a good idea. After you double-click an icon and activate it, the icon changes yet again — this time the small picture changes to an outline filled with small dots.

The Trash icon in the lower-right corner of your desktop is a special icon — you use it to *delete* files and applications from your iMac. Just click and drag a file's icon on top of the Trash icon until the Trash icon changes color, and then release the mouse button. The file disappears from wherever it was on your desktop and reappears in the Trash. (You need to double-click the Trash to look inside and see the file.)

For now, avoid "trashing" anything until you better understand how things work. You don't want to accidentally delete a file you may need later.

Finding Files with Sherlock

All this talk of files and I haven't even told you what files *really* are yet! In the simplest terms, a *file* is an all-encompassing word for a unit of data on your iMac. Most files are either *applications* (program files) or *documents* (files created by applications). You find most files in folders on your hard drive, though you can also find files on your desktop and in menus.

Finding one file on your hard drive can be a daunting task. If you just go around double-clicking folders to find a file, you may eventually find what you're looking for, but it may take forever. Using Sherlock to find a specific file is the quick and easy way.

Sherlock is a special application that searches your hard drive. Here's how to use Sherlock:

1. Pull down the File menu and choose Find. Alternately, you can select it from the Apple menu (look for Sherlock) or you can press and hold the ⌘ key and press the F key — this is called a *keyboard shortcut*. The Sherlock

window appears immediately (see Figure 2-3), ready for you to type in a word or phrase that matches (in part or whole) the file's name.

Figure 2-3: Sherlock detects files.

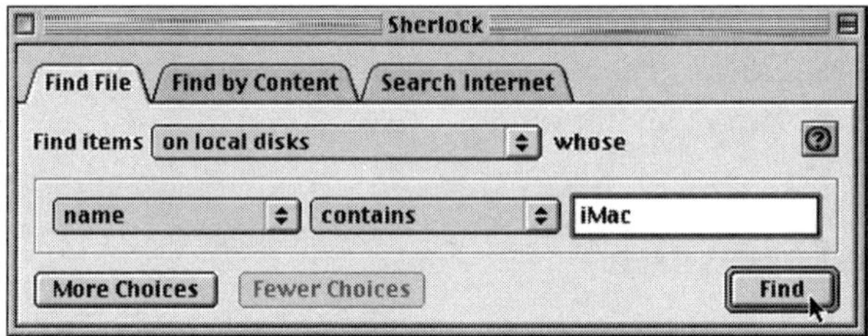

2. Start typing at any time. The blinking *insertion point* is your visual clue that the box accepts typing.
3. After you finish typing, click Find (or press the Return key) and Sherlock searches for your word or phrase. If Sherlock finds matches for your word or phrase, a new window appears listing the item(s) found.
4. Click once on any name to get a hierarchical view of that item's location on your hard drive. You can now double-click to open any item displayed in the window. If you want to open the folder an item resides in, double-click the folder itself in the hierarchical view. (You can open any other folder you see, too.)

Using the Control Strip

The *Control Strip* is the bar at the bottom of your desktop — the one with all the little icons and arrows. It comes enabled on your iMac right out of the box. The Control Strip provides shortcuts to many of the menu items (and submenu items) on your iMac.

Most new iMac users first notice how much the Control Strip gets in the way. After all, the Control Strip is always visible, even if you attempt to cover it with other windows. If you want to minimize it for now and return to it later, you can either click the small Close box at the left end or the tab at the right end. Doing this leaves just the tab sticking out, which you can click again to view the entire Control Strip.

If you want to remove the Control Strip completely from your screen, pull down the Apple menu, display the Control Panels submenu, choose Control Strip, and click the Hide Control Strip radio button.

Setting Preferences

The iMac enables you to customize the look and feel of the desktop a bit. You can specify your settings (*preferences*) in a variety of places for a variety of things.

Changing your desktop preferences

To set your basic desktop preferences, follow these steps:

1. Pull down the Edit menu and choose Preferences at the bottom. A new window for your preference settings opens on your desktop (see Figure 2-4). At the top of the window are three tabs: General, Views, and Labels.

Figure 2-4: Set your desktop preferences.

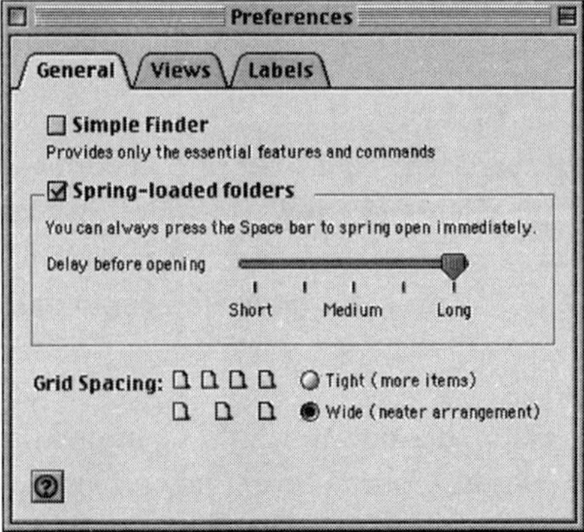

2. Click the General tab if it's behind one of the other two. Here are the preferences you can adjust:

   Simple Finder, which is a stripped-down version of the desktop (that is, fewer menu items). I don't recommend that you enable this right now, because you may not be able to find menu items later in the book.

   Spring-loaded folders, which means that folders open automatically when you drag something onto them. Uncheck the box next to this option if folders popping open suddenly bother you. If you like the option, keep it checked and consider adjusting the delay-before-opening time.

   Grid Spacing, which enables you to choose how your icons line up on the desktop: Choose Tight if you want to fit more or keep Wide if you want your icons in neat, tidy columns.

3. Click the Views tab at the top to choose settings that effect how icons and such in your windows appear.
4. Select the view that you want to modify from the drop-down menu and click the appropriate options. Here are the different views:

   Icons view arranges and sizes icons — the Control Panels window back in Figure 2-2 was in icons view, for example.

   Buttons view arranges and sizes buttons.

   List view offers even more options. Feel free to experiment with these.

5. Click the Labels tab to designate colors and categories for your icons to help you organize things in windows.

Using the View menu

You may notice that many options under the View menu seem similar to those in your desktop preferences. They are, with one important exception: Changes made to windows via the View menu only affect the active window, not all windows. Use the View Menu when you want to change only the organization of your current window.

Using your Control Panels

Another huge group of settings is your Control Panels (located under the Apple menu). *Control Panels* enable you to set preferences for your iMac. The Control Panels that affect the desktop are as follows:

- Appearance
- Date & Time
- General Controls
- Launcher
- Monitors & Sound

You may not be sure what may (or may not) work best for you. If you're unsure, try using the normal (or *default*) preferences for a while to see how you like them.

CHAPTER 3
CONNECTING TO THE INTERNET

IN THIS CHAPTER

- Understanding the Internet
- Connecting your iMac
- Using America Online
- Using Internet service providers

The Internet. You hear about it on the radio, on TV, and in the papers. The buzz is on the street, around the dining room table, and in the office. You hear grandiose claims about how it can change your life, or at least how you can find great deals on it. What is it?

The *Internet* is a vast network of computers all over the world. It's amazingly diverse and rich, offering information and resources beyond your imagination. And wouldn't you know, your iMac connects to the Internet quickly and easily.

Virtually everything you need to connect comes with your iMac. You need only to set up your iMac, sign up for your connection service, and access the Internet. In this chapter, you prepare your iMac for the Internet and then make the connection via America Online or an Internet service provider.

Understanding the Internet

Before you get into the specifics of connecting to the Internet, you need to understand the Internet itself. Not everyone needs or wants to connect to the Internet, even if it has become all the rage. You don't need to be connected to the Internet to use or make the most of your iMac. Most folks, including myself, are interested in the Internet, but if you aren't, feel free to skip ahead!

The Internet is rarely what people think it is. First, it isn't a new phenomenon — it has been around since the 1960s when the military set it up. Second, no one entity owns or administers the Internet — it is a system of individually owned and operated computers linked to one another in a vast "web" around the world. Third, it isn't total anarchy. Millions of computers communicate with one another through the Internet, and that requires some sort of organization. You'll actually think of the Internet as an orderly place, after you know how it works.

Another common misconception is that things like e-mail and the World Wide Web *are* the Internet. In fact, they are only aspects of the Internet, albeit popular ones. For those of you who are unfamiliar with those terms, *e-mail* (which stands for *electronic mail*) is a way to send messages back and forth to other computers connected to the Internet. The *World Wide Web* is a way of displaying information on the Internet. I show you other aspects of the Internet you may not have been aware of later in the book.

Connecting to the Internet requires the following items:

- The right equipment — your iMac has everything a computer needs to connect.
- A standard telephone line — odds are, you already have one of those.
- The right software applications — again, your iMac includes such software on its hard drive.
- A connection to the Internet — the software applications on your iMac can help you establish a connection.

Connecting Your iMac

Before you can actually connect to the Internet, you need to connect your iMac! Your iMac comes with a telephone line cable. If you didn't already attach this, now is the time to do so. One end goes in the telephone line jack behind your iMac's access door (on the right side) and the other goes into a standard telephone wall jack.

If your telephone line cable doesn't stretch all the way to your wall jack, you can buy a longer cable at a hardware store.

The telephone line cable is for the built-in modem inside your iMac. A *modem* is a device that translates the digital information on your iMac into signals that can be sent across standard telephone lines, and vice versa. Your iMac has a *56K* modem, which is a pretty fast modem! In fact, you'll be lucky to achieve 56K speeds even with a 56K modem — not all telephone lines are "clean" enough to support these transfer speeds. (By clean, I mean a telephone line free of static, pops, and hisses that are relatively innocuous in voice calls but deadly in data transfers.) The faster your modem, the more you can transmit through it.

Now that you have the equipment, you need the software. You have two different kinds of Internet software already on your iMac: America Online and EarthLink Total Access. Both offer a connection to the Internet, but they differ in what they offer beyond that. Here's the skinny on each:

- **America Online** is an *online service,* a self-contained place that connects you to the Internet in a safe, user-friendly way. I recommend America Online for beginners and those who want a more cohesive community.
- **EarthLink Total Access** is an *Internet service provider* (ISP), which simply connects you to the Internet; you're on your own after that. An ISP works better for those

who've used ISPs before or are mostly interested in the World Wide Web.

The following sections offer a closer look at each.

Using America Online

America Online is the world's most popular online service with over 17 million members currently. America Online, or "AOL" as it's more commonly called, offers Internet access *plus* easy-to-use e-mail, discussion groups, chats, downloadable files, and more! AOL is not a free service, however — prices range from a few bucks a month for limited service to $10–$25 for unlimited service. You can try AOL for free for 100 hours before you plunk down your hard-earned money. Check your Accessory Kit that came with your iMac for a flyer from AOL.

Setting up America Online

To sign up for the AOL service, follow these steps:

1. Double-click the Macintosh HD icon on your desktop, open the Internet folder, and then double-click the America Online icon. The America Online icon is actually an *alias,* which means it's just a shortcut to the actual software. Double-clicking it opens it just as if you double-clicked the actual software icon.
2. The America Online software loads quickly and then welcomes you! The Setup window guides you through the setup process, much like the way the Mac OS Setup Assistant helped you set up your iMac in Chapter 1.
3. Click the Next button in the lower-right corner of the window to continue (see Figure 3-1). AOL Setup searches your iMac for a way to connect you — the software looks for a modem, which you have. The Setup window displays the results of its search.

Figure 3-1: Setup is easy with America Online.

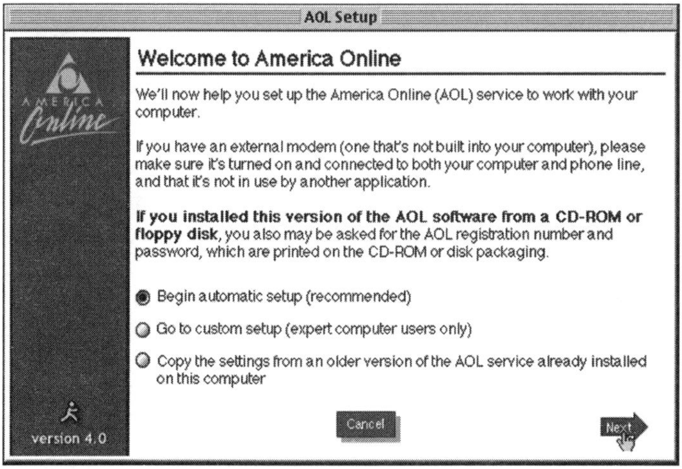

4. Confirm the search results by clicking Next to continue.

5. Confirm your dialing options — click the appropriate check box, if necessary.

6. Click Next again, type your area code in the box, and click Next to begin searching for an access number. Remember that your modem uses the telephone line and thus needs a local telephone number (or two) to dial. The program connects to AOL via a toll-free number to find local access numbers.

7. Make sure no one else is using the telephone line, and then click Next to begin. If a dialog box informs you that your must activate AOL Link, you can safely click OK.

8. When AOL connects to search for access numbers, a progress box pops up and displays each step of the connection process. It works the same way when you connect to AOL for real. You can even hear your modem dial and AOL's modem reply to it, if your speaker volume is turned up loud enough. When the search is complete, AOL hangs up and displays the available access numbers.

8. If you see a phone number in your city or a nearby city, select it (highlight it) and click the Add button to use it. Try to find at least two local numbers — that way, if one is busy, you can use the other.

9. If none of the numbers listed are free local calls, choose nearby numbers — you're responsible for the toll charges. If that's the case, you may be better off finding an Internet service provider that can provide a no-cost local access number. Click Cancel if you want to stop the setup process now.

10. Click Next to continue. AOL uses your new access numbers to dial the service and connect. You're now ready to create your America Online account.

11. If, by chance, you already have an AOL account or are an AOL Instant Messenger user, click the appropriate radio button. Otherwise, click Next to continue on and type your name, address, and telephone numbers.

12. Continue through the setup process to provide your billing information (credit cards or checking account withdrawal), and then select your screen name and password. Your *screen name* is also your e-mail address, so choose wisely. Your *password* should be a combination of letters and numbers that are not easy to guess.

That's all there is to it! If you have problems with any step of this setup process, you can call AOL at 1-888-265-8007 for assistance.

Making the most of America Online

After you make it onto America Online, take a few minutes to poke around and explore. AOL has a lot to offer, though, so don't be surprised if it all seems a bit overwhelming. Visit the new member area to learn more about AOL — just click the "Yes, Let's get started"! button on the Welcome to AOL window (see Figure 3-2).

Figure 3-2: America Online helps you get started quickly.

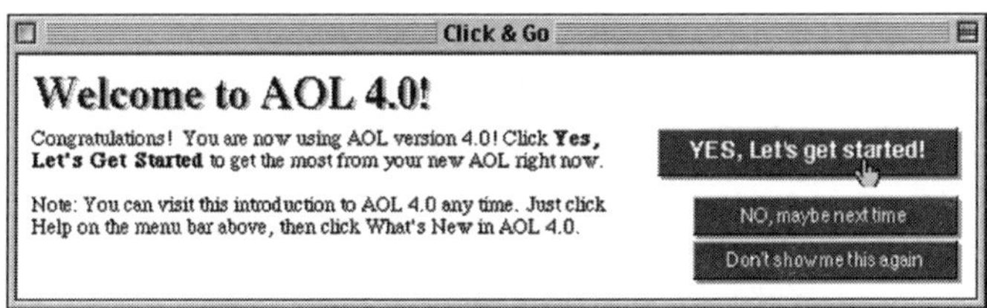

Using Internet Service Providers

EarthLink TotalAccess is the iMac's Internet service provider (ISP) of choice. If you already have a local ISP you prefer to use, you certainly can do that! EarthLink is a national ISP, so it works for everyone, just about anywhere. EarthLink isn't a free service either — it costs about 20 bucks per month to connect. An additional hourly charge may be added to use the toll-free number if you can't find a local number to use.

EarthLink doesn't offer local access numbers for many places. You may wind up paying more for EarthLink access than for AOL access.

Setting up an ISP

Unlike America Online, some ISPs don't provide their own setup software. Here's how to set up your iMac to use EarthLink:

1. Double-click the Macintosh HD icon on your desktop, open the Internet folder, and double-click Internet Setup Assistant.
2. Click Yes when Internet Setup Assistant asks you if you want to set up your iMac to use the Internet. (Tough question, huh?)
3. If you already have an ISP account, click Yes in the next window — otherwise click No. If you clicked Yes, skip down to the section "Establishing a Connection to an

Existing ISP." If you clicked No, read the agreement displayed in the resulting window carefully and then click I Agree (assuming you do).

4. In the TotalAccess welcome window, choose to either set up a new account (click this if you're new to EarthLink) or retrieve an EarthLink account (if you already have one). Clicking Setup prompts you to choose a user name and password (see Figure 3-3).

Figure 3-3: Type in a user name and password.

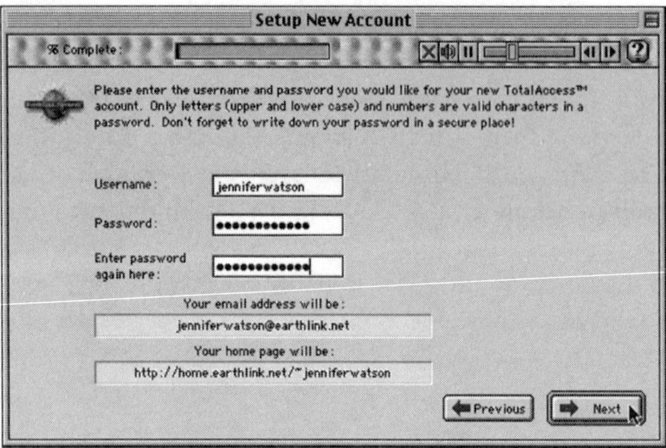

5. Choose a good user name because it becomes the first part of your e-mail address. Choose a difficult-to-guess password that is a combination of both letters and numbers.

6. Click Next to continue setting up your account. The rest of the setup process is self-explanatory.

When you complete your EarthLink setup, the software connects you to the Internet. Answer a few more questions and you're finished. If you encounter problems, call EarthLink at 1-800-395-8410 for assistance.

Establishing a connection to an existing ISP

If you already have an ISP account (other than EarthLink), Internet Setup Assistant can help you set it up on your new iMac. Before you can properly set up your connection, you need some information about your existing ISP account. Specifically, you need to know the following:

- Your ISP's access phone number
- Your user name (different than your e-mail address)
- Your password
- Whether your ISP requires a "PPP connect script" (and what it is)
- Whether or not an IP address exists (and, if so, what it is)
- The domain name servers (DNS addresses)
- Your e-mail address and the password for it
- The e-mail account host names (POP and SMTP)
- The newsgroup host name (NNTP)
- Whether or not your ISP uses proxy servers

Unless you're a superhero, you can't remember all this information. Call your ISP first, write down the answers to the questions above, and then continue through the setup process with the Internet Setup Assistant.

Setting Your Internet Preferences

One last task remains: your Internet preferences. You could probably go straight to the Internet without setting them, but you'll encounter far fewer snags if you set them first. I recommend you set your preferences whether you're using America Online or an ISP. Here's how:

1. To find your preferences, choose Apple menu⇨Control Panels⇨Internet. You could also click the Internet Alias icon in the same folder you found America Online and Internet Setup Assistant. The preferences window appears (see Figure 3-4).

Figure 3-4: Set your Internet preferences.

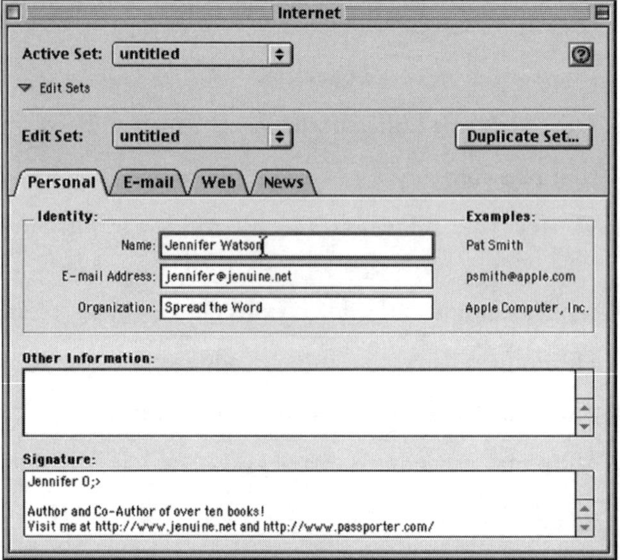

2. Click the E-mail tab to access your e-mail preferences. Using an ISP? Choose Outlook Express for the Default E-mail Application at the bottom of the window. Using AOL? Choose Select... from the drop-down menu at the bottom of the window and locate the America Online application (Macintosh HD⇨Internet⇨Internet⇨America Online).

3. Click the Web tab. If you're using an ISP, choose Microsoft Internet Explorer or Netscape Navigator from the menu at the bottom of the window (Default Web Browser).

Using Outlook Express for your e-mail? It's a good idea to use Microsoft Internet Explorer; they work hand-in-hand. Using AOL? Choose America Online from the menu instead.

You can set other preferences here, too. When you finish, click the Close box and save your changes when prompted.

CHAPTER 4

SURFING THE WEB

IN THIS CHAPTER

- Using Web browsers
- Finding information
- Saving favorite places
- Downloading files
- Staying safe

You view the *World Wide Web* (or just *Web*), that vast and varied quilt of Internet resources, through a special application: the *Web browser*. This application interprets and presents all sorts of Internet information for you, including text, graphics, sound, and video. You don't need to know how to program or be technically oriented to use the Web. Your Web browser does virtually everything for you!

In this chapter, you learn how to use your Web browser, whether you're accessing the Internet through America Online or an ISP. Then you *surf* the Web for information (and find what you seek!), save your findings, and *download* (retrieve) files. Most importantly, you learn how to protect yourself and your computer while you surf the Web.

Using Web Browsers

Your iMac comes with three different Web browsers: America Online's built-in Web browser, Netscape Navigator, and Microsoft Internet Explorer.

While you can use all three browsers, you don't need to use them all, nor do I recommend it. Instead, pick the one that works best for your type of Internet access. America Online users probably want to stick with the Web browser built-in to the AOL software — it's actually a customized version of Microsoft Internet Explorer. ISP users can choose between Netscape Navigator and Microsoft Internet Explorer.

To open a Web browser, double-click the Browse the Internet icon on your desktop (see Figure 4-1).

Figure 4-1: Browse the Internet launches your Web browser.

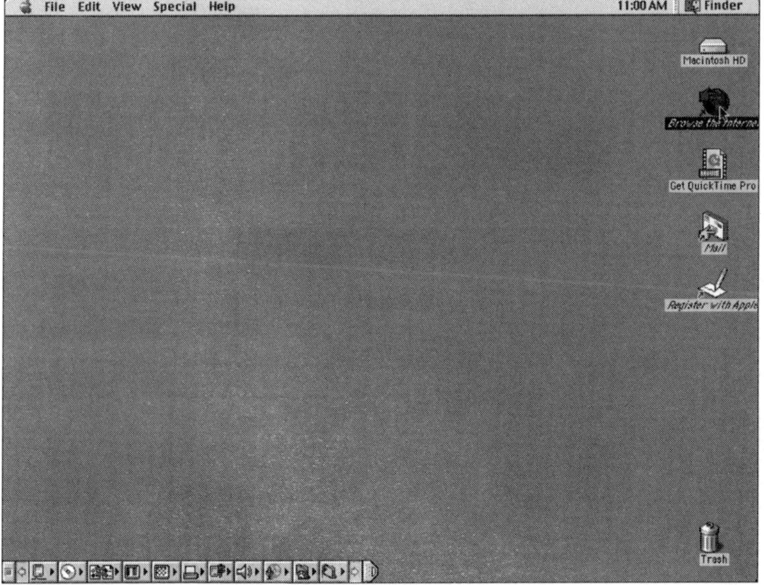

If you don't see the icon, just choose Apple menu⇨Internet Access⇨Browse the Internet. You may be asked again if you are set up to use the Internet (click Yes). If all works as planned, one of two things happens: the AOL software opens (if you are an AOL user) or either Netscape Navigator or Internet Explorer opens, depending on your choice earlier (if you are an ISP user).

How did it know which Web browser you needed? You told your iMac at the end of Chapter 3 when you chose a Web browser in your Internet preferences! If it didn't work out this way, refer back to Chapter 3 to reset your default Web browser.

America Online's Web browser

Before you can use America Online's Web browser, you need to first *sign on* (connect to AOL). Type your screen name and password when prompted, and then click Sign On (or press Return) to connect. After you connect, click the Internet icon on the AOL toolbar and select Go to the Web from the menu. A large windows opens, welcoming you to AOL.COM, AOL's own *Web site,* which is also called their *home page* (see Figure 4-2).

Figure 4-2: AOL's Web browser window displaying the AOL.COM Web site.

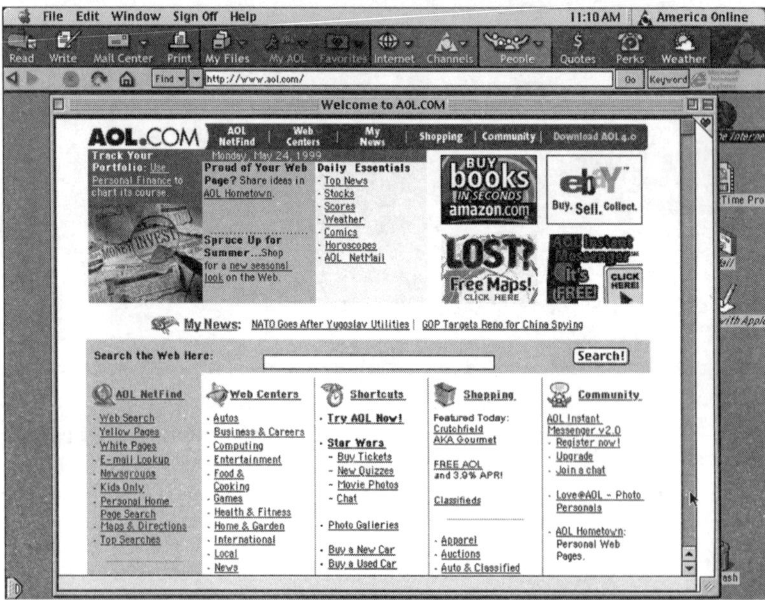

AOL's Web browser controls are at the far left of the AOL toolbar, which is located at the top of the screen below the menu bar. Here's what each browser control does:

- The arrows move you forward and backward through the Web pages you've accessed. (These buttons don't do anything now because you haven't gone anywhere yet!)
- The circle with the *X* cancels an action.
- The circular arrow *reloads* a page (or downloads all the page's elements again).
- The little house returns you to your default Web page.

Skip now to the "Navigating the Web" section, unless you're also interested in using Netscape Navigator or Microsoft Internet Explorer along with AOL's Web browser.

Netscape Navigator

The first time Netscape Navigator opens, it prompts you to set up a new profile — just follow the directions and enter your personal information. In short order, the Web browser window opens and your iMac automatically dials and connects to your ISP. Your default Web page appears. (The default Web page is a special version of the Excite Web search page and directory.)

If you changed your Internet preferences to display no default Web page, you need to type in a Web address (more about Web addresses later) and press Return, or choose an item from the Bookmarks menu, before your iMac connects you to your ISP.

Netscape Navigator's browser controls are at the top of the window. Here's what they do:

- **Back** and **Forward** move you backward and forward through the Web pages you've accessed. (These are grayed out the first time you use the browser.)
- **Reload** downloads the current Web page again, updating the page since you last downloaded it.
- **Home** returns you to the default Web page.
- **Search** helps you find things on the Internet.
- **Guide** is a menu offering shortcuts to some other helpful Web pages.
- **Images** load a Web page's images (if you disabled them in your Netscape preferences).
- **Security** indicates the level of security on a given page.
- **Stop** aborts the loading of a Web page.

Skip now to the "Navigating the Web" section, unless you're also interested in using Microsoft Internet Explorer.

Microsoft Internet Explorer

Upon launching Microsoft Internet Explorer (often abbreviated IE or Internet Explorer), your iMac automatically dials into and connects you to your ISP, and the default Web page appears.

Several toolbars at the top of the browser window offer navigational buttons. Here's what those buttons do:

- **Back** and **Forward** move you through Web pages you've already accessed. (These buttons don't do anything when you first launch the browser.)
- **Stop** aborts the loading of a Web page.
- **Refresh** reloads your current page (just like Reload in Navigator).

- **Home** returns you to the default Web page.
- **Favorites** offers shortcuts to Web pages.
- **History** shows a list of recently visited Web pages.
- **Search** finds things on the Internet.
- **Autofill** automatically completes a Web address after you start typing it.
- **Larger** and **Smaller** zoom in and zoom out on the page.
- **Print** gives you a paper copy of the Web page you're reading.
- **Mail** takes you to either Outlook Express (covered in the next chapter) or America Online, depending on which e-mail application you specified in your Internet preferences.
- **Preferences** offer settings to customize your browser.
- The **globe buttons** below the toolbar offer more shortcuts.
- The **tabs** on the left side of the window "pull out" to offer even more shortcuts — if you accidentally pull out a tab, just click on the tab again to put it away.

Navigating the Web

Although you can visualize the interconnected computers of the Internet as a web, the thing that makes the World Wide Web such an amazing tool is a simple concept — the *hypertext link,* or *hyperlink*. A World Wide Web document (page) is designed so that it can fetch other useful Web pages, documents, images, sounds, or whatever, from anywhere else on the Internet. In fact, each page you see displayed on your computer screen may be made up of many pieces — text, images, sounds — all fetched one at a time from computers on the Internet. Not only can a Web page tell you, "For further information, read the following...," you can access the information directly with one click of a blue, underlined hypertext link. When you access that piece of information, you may find hypertext links to still more information, and so on.

As you wander through this world of information, all those random interconnections begin to look like a web. You may also get lost. That's where the *navigation buttons* come in. The Forward and Back buttons on your browser enable you to backtrack, if you've gone down a dead end, or move forward again, if you've backtracked too far. Because it takes time for your browser to display each page, the Stop button can save time when you know you've followed the wrong link. Sometimes, especially when a page is made up of many pieces, the page doesn't display properly. The Reload button lets you try again (and again).

You can use the scroll bars (if active) to move up and down or side to side through a Web page. Sometimes, icons and pictures within a Web page have hyperlinks attached to them; clicking them can take you to other pages, too. If you're not sure which items on a Web page you can click, move your pointer over words and pictures — when your pointer changes to a hand, this is a visual clue that you can click it to go somewhere else. Also, as your pointer hovers over the link, notice that the *Web address* of a page appears in the lower-left corner of your browser window. This information can help if you're not sure whether you want to click something.

A Web address looks like gobbledygook, but it really does mean something. The string of letters and symbols (and sometimes numbers) in the text box near the top of your Web browser is the address of the current Web page. It generally starts with `http://` and has a lot of slashes (/) in it. These addresses, also called URLs (Uniform Resource Locators — don't worry about what it stands for!), are what you and your browser use to navigate the Web. Note that URLs are different than e-mail addresses. Hyperlinks and buttons provide the URL to your browser, but you can also type the URL directly into the text box. When you type in a URL, you don't have to type the `http://` part; your browser fills that in for you.

If you want to try a new URL, use this one:

```
www.jenuine.net
```

Type it just as you see it, and then press the Return key to activate it. Your browser looks up the address and displays the information. This URL leads to my Web page, and you're welcome to look around while you get used to your Web browser.

Finding Information on the Web

Wondering how to find what you want in this sea of information? The Web *can* be overwhelming, even to experienced Web surfers. Unless you know exactly where you want to go (and have the URL to it), the best way to find something on the Web is to search for it.

The easiest way to search for something is to use the Search feature. Each of the three Web browsers we explore in this chapter have a built-in Search button. In AOL's browser, click Find (next to the Home button) and select Find it on the Web. In Netscape Navigator or Microsoft Internet Explorer, click Search (see Figure 4-3).

Though the specific search page that these browsers use may differ from one another, they have common elements. Follow these general steps to search for something on the Web:

1. To begin a search, type a word or phrase into the text entry box in the Web page (not the text entry box at the top of the browser). Be specific and check your spelling.

Figure 4-3: Searching the Web in Microsoft Internet Explorer.

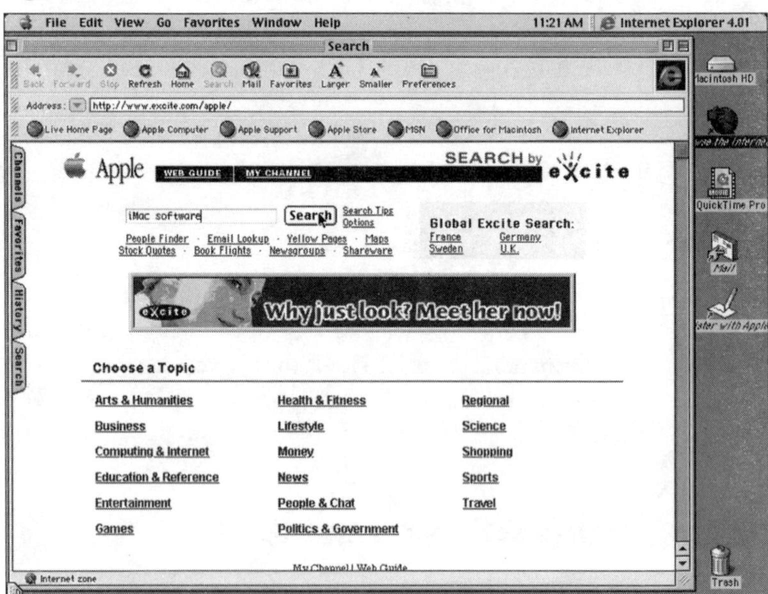

2. Click Search, usually found to the right of the text entry box. Your Web browser goes to work immediately. Note that the picture in the upper-right corner is animated while your browser is searching — this is a visual clue that something is happening (and it isn't finished yet). When your search is complete, your Web browser displays the results in order of relevancy.

3. If you see a good match, click the hyperlink to go to that page. If you don't get good results, you may need to search on more specific words or phrases.

You may also want to try other Web directories, such as Yahoo! (`www.yahoo.com`) or Lycos (`www.lycos.com`).

Another technique to find a particular Web site is to *guess* a URL. For example, if you're planning a trip to Walt Disney World, you could just type `www.waltdisneyworld.com`

(it works!). Almost every major company and organization has a Web site these days, and they generally have easy addresses. Just type **www.**, the company or organization name, and then **.com** — you'll be surprised at how often this works. In fact, in Netscape Navigator and Internet Explorer, you can just get away with typing the company or organization name — the browser fills in the `http://www.` and `.com` for you!

Saving Favorite Places

When you find what you're looking for, save it! Each Web browser offers a way to save favorite places (or *bookmarks*) so that you can return to the page again without having to hunt it down.

All addresses you save in your Web browser stay on the list of favorites or bookmarks until you remove them. They remain even after you quit your Web browser and disconnect from the Internet.

Saving a favorite place in AOL's browser

See the little red heart in the upper-right corner of your AOL Web browser window? Click it once, and confirm that you want to add the page to your Favorite Places. To return to this page in the future, just click the Favorite Places icon on the AOL toolbar and select the page from the menu. Alternately, you can select Favorite Places from that menu to display a Favorite Places window, and then select the page from there. Note that you can organize your favorite places into folders and subfolders, too!

Saving a bookmark in Netscape Navigator

To save an address, pull down the Bookmarks menu in the menu bar (with the bookmark icon) and choose Add Bookmark (or press ⌘+D). Alternately, you can double-click the smaller bookmark icon to the left of the URL text box. Now, you can return to this page by selecting it from the bottom of the Bookmark menu (see Figure 4-4). To organize your bookmarks into folders, press ⌘+B to display the Bookmarks window.

Figure 4-4: Netscape Navigator stores your favorite Web sites.

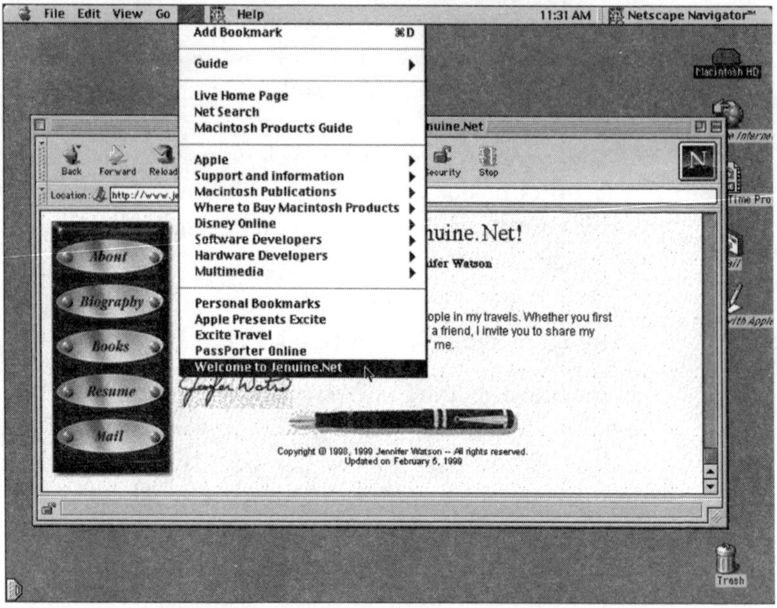

Saving a favorite in Microsoft Internet Explorer

To save an address, pull down the Favorites menu and choose Add Page to Favorites (or just press ⌘+D). Now you can choose it from your Favorites menu at anytime. You can also access your favorites by clicking the Favorites tab on the left of your browser window. The window splits in two, showing your list of favorites on the left and the current Web page on the right. Note that you can also open the Favorites window, where you can organize your favorites into folders, by choosing Favorites⇨Edit Favorites.

Downloading Files

Downloading is the process of transferring information to your iMac from another computer (usually one on the Internet). As you surf the Web, you download information that your Web browser displays for you.

You can find files to download all over the Web — in fact, you may not even realize that there is a file to download until it begins downloading! Sometimes, a download happens in the "background" and your only indication that a download is taking place is the messages in the lower-left corner of your browser window. You can cancel a download at anytime by clicking Cancel or pressing ⌘+(period).

Before you download any file, please read the next section, "Staying Safe." I wouldn't want you to catch a virus!

A great source of files to download is `www.shareware.com`, which has over 250,000 files. Shareware is a file (usually an application) that you can download for free; if you decide to keep it, you pay a fee.

Web sites often offer files to download, either for free or for purchase. For example, Apple's Web site (`www.apple.com`) offers helpful utilities and upgrades to its software — even games for your iMac!

When you're ready to download, click the Download button or the hyperlink for the file. Upon initiating a download, you're usually asked where you want to place the file on your hard drive. You can use the default location or pick a new place — just make a note of it for later! After the download is complete, you can switch to your desktop and find it there, like any other file. Double-click the file to open or install it.

Staying Safe

All this talk of the Internet, the Web, and downloading files brings up the issue of safety. Horror stories abound about the wild and dangerous Internet. Safety on the Internet is much like safety in your everyday life: It's a matter of common sense. Here are some tips for safe surfing:

- **To protect your AOL or ISP account, safeguard your password.** Never give your password to anyone, even if they claim to be from an authority like AOL or the ISP itself.

Be careful not to leave your password where anyone can find it, either. Don't write it on a piece of paper and stick it under your keyboard. Memorize your password, or use a code only you understand. Choose passwords carefully — use both letters and numbers, make them long, and make them hard to guess. Also, change your password regularly — try once a month.

- **To protect your iMac from a computer virus, get a virus protection program and install it.** The two major virus protection applications for the Mac are Norton AntiVirus (`www.symantec.com`) and Virex (`www.drsolomon.com`).
- **Be mindful of your surroundings much as you would be anywhere else.** If you do decide to send sensitive information across the Web, be sure you're on a "secure" page where a third party can't intercept information.

CHAPTER 5

DOING E-MAIL

IN THIS CHAPTER

- Reading e-mail
- Writing e-mail
- Sending e-mail
- Attaching files to e-mail
- Automating e-mail
- Protecting yourself and your e-mail

E-mail (short for *electronic mail*) is taking the world by storm! If you're not yet familiar with this new form of communication, you're in for a treat. It's fast, efficient, and fun! With it, you can exchange messages with someone, whether he's down the road or around the world in the same amount of time . . . (and for the same amount of money.)

In this chapter, you learn how to read your e-mail, write a reply, and send it. You also discover how you can attach a file (like a photo or an application) to an e-mail so that it can piggyback along with your message. You find tips to help you manage and automate all the e-mail you'll soon be receiving. Finally, you learn how to protect yourself from danger and safeguard your e-mail from loss.

Reading E-mail

Even if you just got your Internet access through AOL or an ISP, chances are very good that you already have e-mail waiting for you. Have you read it yet? Do you have any idea who it might be from (hint: AOL and most ISPs send a welcome e-mail to new subscribers)? Not sure where to start? Just double-click the Mail icon on your desktop (or choose it from the Internet Access submenu under the Apple menu). Your e-mail application — be it America Online or Outlook Express — opens for you. If America Online opens, keep reading. If Outlook Express opens instead, skip down a bit.

Reading e-mail on America Online

America Online's e-mail system is easy and friendly. To check your e-mail, first sign on and AOL tells you whether you have mail with its now-famous "You've got mail" announcement. You can also locate the mailbox icon on the toolbar or Welcome screen. If you have e-mail, the little red flag on the mailbox will be up (and a smaller version of the mailbox flashes on and off in the upper-right corner of your desktop). If you have e-mail, click the mailbox icon on your toolbar or your Welcome screen. Your Online Mailbox window opens and displays all your new e-mail (see Figure 5-1).

Figure 5-1: Your mailbox on America Online.

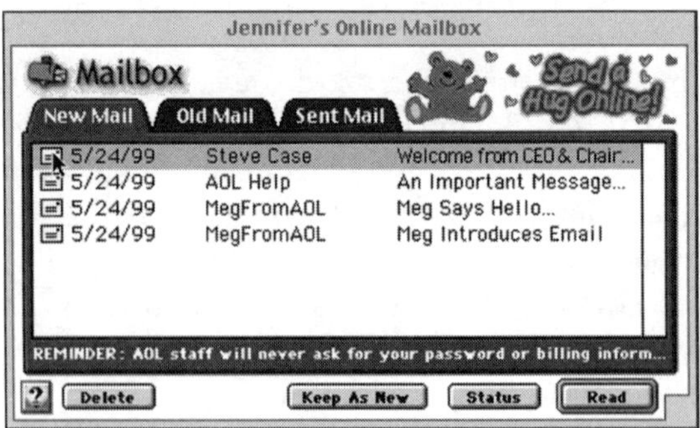

To read a piece of e-mail, select it in your mailbox and click Read (or just double-click it). Another window opens, displaying the address of the sender, the subject of the e-mail, the date sent, and the message itself.

The sender's address immediately tells you if the person is using AOL or is elsewhere on the Internet. Regular Internet e-mail addresses have these three parts:

- A user name
- An @ symbol
- A domain name, which is equivalent to the city, state, and country on a normal letter

Because all AOL members "live" in the same domain, you need only the member's user name (or *screen name*) when you send e-mail to or receive e-mail from that member. I'm "Jennifer" to other AOL members, and `Jennifer@aol.com` to the rest of the Internet.

When you finish reading an e-mail, you can do several things:

- You can click one of the arrows near the top of the e-mail window to move forward or backward through your list of e-mail.
- You can click Delete to clear it from your e-mail list entirely (only do this if you really don't want to ever see it again).
- You can click the Close box in the upper-left corner.
- You can click the Reply, Forward, or Reply All buttons, which I discuss a little later.

Reading e-mail with your ISP

If you have an ISP, your e-mail opens automatically when you double-click the Mail button on your desktop (see Figure 5-2).

Figure 5-2: Outlook Express works with your ISP e-mail account.

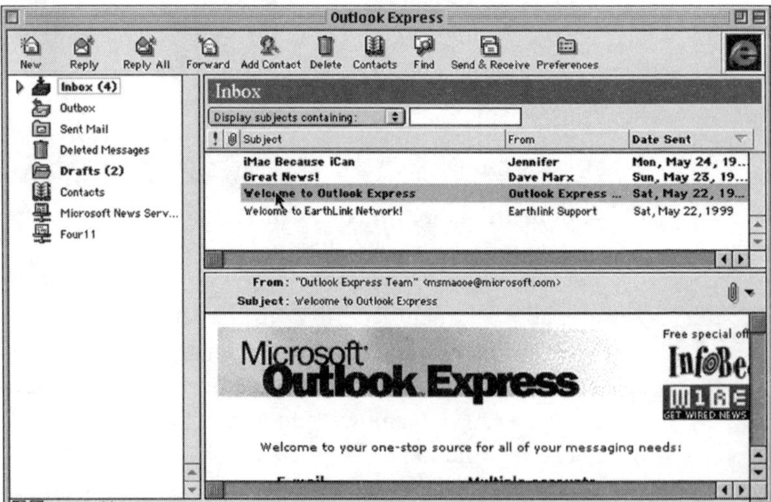

Any new e-mail is listed in your Inbox. Messages in boldface indicate they are brand new and unread. Click once on a message to view it in the bottom half of your Outlook Express window. Double-click a message to view it in its own window.

If you read an e-mail in its own window, you can use the arrows in the upper-left corner to move backward and forward through your e-mail list. You can click Delete to remove the e-mail from your Inbox permanently, or just click the Close box to close the window (but not delete the e-mail). Alternately, you can click the Reply, Reply All, or Forward button to respond to the e-mail.

Writing E-mail

Reading e-mail is only the start. E-mail is a two-way medium, which is what makes it so fun. You can write your own e-mail and reply to the e-mail you receive from others! Here are the three ways of writing e-mail:

- Replying to (or forwarding) an e-mail message you received
- Writing a new e-mail message from scratch
- Clicking an e-mail hyperlink on a Web page

Here, I take a look at each of these options in AOL and Outlook Express!

If you're unsure how to type and compose a letter in e-mail, you may find it helpful to read Chapter 6.

Writing e-mail in America Online

The easiest way to write e-mail is to click the Reply, Reply All, or Forward button on a piece of e-mail you received (see Figure 5-3).

Figure 5-3: A reply e-mail awaits your message.

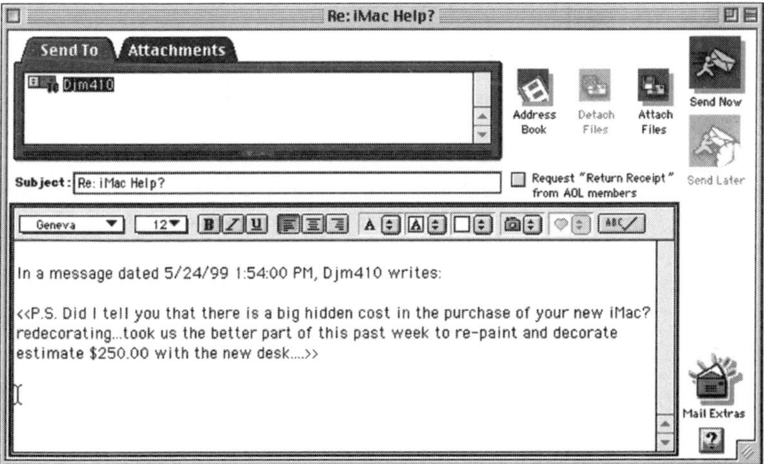

AOL fills in most of the blanks for you automatically, and all you need to do is type the message. Which button is best? Use the following list as your guide:

- Use Reply when you want to send a message only to the person who sent you the e-mail.

- Use Reply All when you want to send a message back to the person who sent you the e-mail and everyone else they sent it to.
- Use Forward if you want to send a copy of the original e-mail you received to someone else or even to the same person (that is, to remind them of what they said).

Highlight some of the text in your e-mail before you click the Reply, Reply All, or Forward button. The text is automatically copied (quoted) in your new e-mail message. Nifty!

To compose a new e-mail message from scratch in AOL, just click the Write icon on the toolbar (or press ⌘+N). You need to fill in the Send To box with the recipient's screen name or Internet e-mail address. Note that you don't need to enter your own e-mail address anywhere — AOL already knows what it is and automatically attaches it to your e-mail when you send it.

Writing e-mail in Outlook Express

Replying to e-mail is simple. Click the Reply or Reply All button and a new message window appears, preaddressed to the recipient(s) of your original e-mail (see Figure 5-4).

Use Reply if you want to send your response only to the person who sent the e-mail. Alternately, use Reply All if you want to send your response to that person and everyone else who received a copy of the same e-mail. Use Forward if you want to send along a copy of the e-mail with your response.

To write a brand new e-mail in Outlook Express, just click New in the upper-left corner of the Outlook Express window. A new, blank message window appears, ready for you to type in the e-mail address (be sure to use the full e-mail address, including the @ symbol), the subject line, and your message. Your own e-mail address is automatically added.

Figure 5-4: Outlook Express makes replies easy, too!

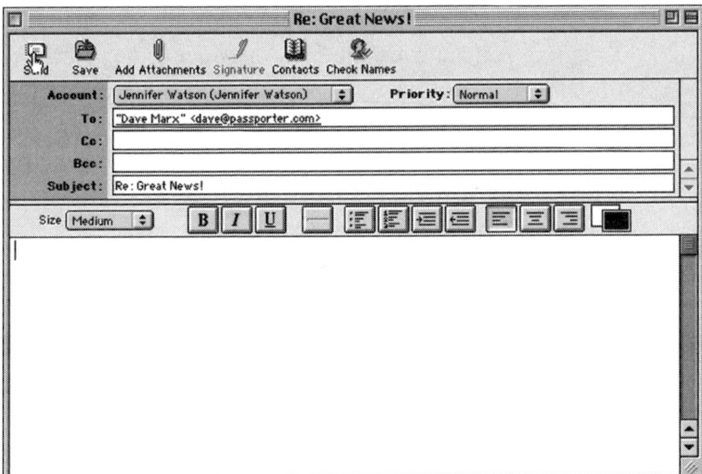

Writing e-mail on the Web

When you surf the Web, you'll undoubtedly come across hyperlinks to e-mail addresses. They may not always say they are e-mail addresses, but even then, you can usually tell because it is a person's name. If you click one of these links, one of two things can happen. A blank message window may open in AOL or Outlook Express (with the recipient's name already filled in). Alternately, a new Web page may open that looks a bit like an e-mail window, complete with a message box. Either one works for sending e-mail, so don't be afraid to try them!

Sending E-mail

After you write your e-mail, you need to get it to your intended recipient by sending it. I always get a kick out of this part. I don't have to go to my mailbox or the post office. I don't have to scrounge for an envelope or a stamp. I don't have to do a lot of things because sending e-mail is incredibly easy: Just click Send.

Of course, you do need to be connected to the Internet (or *online*) when you send your e-mail for it to actually go through. If you aren't online, you can queue your e-mail to send later, after you connect to the Internet. In AOL, just click Send Later — when you get online, go to the Mail Center icon, choose Mail Waiting to be Sent from the menu, and send your waiting e-mail. In Outlook Express, click Save to queue it, and then open the Drafts folder to send it after you're connected.

If you want to check e-mail you've sent, you can! Here's how:

- On AOL, click the Sent Mail tab at the top of your Online Mailbox for a list of all mail you've sent recently.
- In Outlook Express, open the Sent Mail folder for a similar list.

You can open your sent e-mail to see what you sent and when you sent it. You can even *unsend* an e-mail on AOL if your recipient is also on AOL and hasn't yet read it — just select an e-mail and click Unsend at the bottom of the Sent Mail list.

You can try out your e-mail even if you don't have anyone to e-mail yet! Try sending e-mail to yourself (if you've forgotten your e-mail address already, check a piece of sent mail for it). You can also send e-mail to me at my AOL address (`jennifer@aol.com`, or just `Jennifer` if you're on AOL) or my Internet address (`jennifer@jenuine.net`). I will reply, too!

Attaching Files to E-mail

Another wonderfully useful feature of e-mail is the ability to attach a file to e-mail. This is a bit like getting free package delivery for the price of a 33-cent stamp. You can use this feature to send a picture of your new dog, a file with your award-winning report on butterflies, a sound recording of your baby's first words, or the latest shareware game! You can even use e-mail to send files to yourself when you're traveling, or just to keep a record off your computer (for privacy or security). You're limited only by the size of your file and your imagination.

Keep in mind that the larger the attachment, the longer the attachment takes to travel across the Internet. Expect longer upload times for large files.

Attaching files to AOL e-mail

To attach a file to an e-mail in America Online, first open a new, blank message window or reply to an e-mail you received. Now click the Attach Files button near the top right of the window. Select the file (or folder) you want to attach. If you select a folder, AOL automatically *compresses* your folder into one file to make it easier and smaller to send. You can add more than one file or folder, too — just click Attach Files again to add more. If you want to remove a file, just select it from the list at the top of the window and click Detach Files. Click Send when you're ready to send your e-mail and attached file. If your file is large, AOL keeps you up-to-date on the progress of the file transfer from your iMac to AOL's computers. You can attach files up to 16MB (megabytes) in size.

Attaching files to Outlook Express e-mail

In Outlook Express, click Add Attachments in a new e-mail message window. Select and add the individual files you want to attach — each one appears in the lower half of the window. If you want to add an entire folder, click the Add All button to include each file in the folder. When you finish adding files, click Done. Icons of the files appear at the bottom of your window — if you want to remove one, just select it and choose Clear from the Edit menu. The size limit of your attached file(s) varies from ISP to ISP — check with them if you're unsure. Outlook Express doesn't automatically compress (reduce the size of) your files — if you want it to do so, choose Preferences from the Edit menu, click Message Composition, and click the check box next to Compress Attachments. When you're ready to send your e-mail with its attached file(s), just click Send — Outlook Express updates you on the file's progress as it transfers from your iMac to your ISP's computers.

Downloading attached files

Just as you can send attached files, you can receive them as well! With AOL e-mail, a floppy disk icon appears when an e-mail has an attached file — just click Download Now to retrieve the file. In Outlook Express, the paper clip icon (Attachments) at the top of a piece of e-mail lets you retrieve your attachments.

Automating E-mail

It won't take long to start getting too much e-mail. E-mail has an uncanny way of stacking up, especially after you start sending out e-mail to others. I get about 500 pieces a day! Don't worry, though — I get more than most people. Still, staying on top of it has taught me a few tricks that I can pass on to you.

- **Take advantage of any e-mail automation features your software may provide.** AOL offers quite a few, including the ability to schedule e-mail "runs" where you can send and receive e-mail in the middle of the night if you wish! To learn more about this, click Mail Center icon and select Set up Automatic AOL. You can also set Outlook Express to connect and check your e-mail as soon as you open it, which is also useful.

- **Use your address book feature.** Both AOL and Outlook Express offer a way to store e-mail addresses. On AOL, save addresses by selecting them and clicking the Remember Address button (or just double-click an address). You can then view your Address Book by choosing Address Book under the Mail Center menu. In Outlook Express, save addresses by choosing Save Sender to Contacts under the Tools menu (or press ⌘+=). View your Contacts by clicking the Address Book icon in a New Mail window.
- **Organize the e-mail you receive.** In AOL, a Personal Filing Cabinet holds folders and e-mail messages. You can also set AOL to save all e-mail you read and send in your Personal Filing Cabinet. You can access your Personal Filing Cabinet under the My Files icon in the toolbar. In Outlook Express, you create folders in your Inbox and Outbox — just pull down the File menu, display the New submenu, and choose Folder (or Subfolder). You can also set Outlook Express to save all e-mail you read and save. In fact, Outlook lets you define "rules" to do certain things to certain e-mail, such as putting it in a particular folder or playing a special sound. Choose Mail Rules from the Tools menu to create a new e-mail rule.

Protecting Yourself and Your E-mail

E-mail has its share of pitfalls. Protect yourself from the unsavory and obnoxious, and protect your e-mail from accidental loss.

When receiving e-mail from people you don't know, be cautious. Don't click on hyperlinks, download any attachments, or open any attached file if you don't know the sender. On AOL, avoid opening e-mail with attached pictures from unknown senders (you can tell by the little flashbulb icon in your mailbox list) — they may contain objectionable or offensive images.

You can screen out dangers automatically, too. On AOL, click the Mail Center icon, choose Mail Controls from the menu, and follow the directions. In Outlook Express, Mail Rules filters objectionable e-mails.

If you read an e-mail but don't have time to reply to it right away, consider "keeping it as new" so it remains in your New Mail or Inbox. To do this on AOL, select the e-mail in your Online Mailbox and click the Keep as New button. In Outlook Express, select the e-mail in your Inbox and choose Message➪Mark as Unread.

If an e-mail is important, save it to your hard drive — select Save or Save As from your File menu while an e-mail window is open. The best way to backup all your saved e-mail in either AOL or Outlook Express is to save a copy of the data files containing the e-mail. (Find the AOL e-mail data files by searching for "Filing Cabinet" in Sherlock. Outlook Express saves its data files in a folder called "OE User(s).") Don't move the original data files when saving a copy. To save a copy, hold down the Option key and click and drag the file or folder to another folder. Alternately, you could save a copy to a Zip disk or floppy disk, if you have these installed and available to you.

CHAPTER 6

WRITING YOUR FIRST LETTER WITH APPLEWORKS

IN THIS CHAPTER

- Using AppleWorks
- Selecting and moving text
- Cutting, copying, and pasting text
- Using Clear and Undo
- Applying fonts and styles
- Saving your work

If you've already typed and sent an e-mail, you may be wondering if you need to read this chapter at all. I have just one question for you: How do you send a letter to someone who isn't connected to the Internet? Like all those people who held off on getting a telephone and then a color TV, not everyone has a computer yet. And those who do aren't all connected to the Internet to receive e-mail. So until we're all one big, Internet-connected family, we still need to write traditional letters. Your iMac not only does traditional letters, but it does them *well!*

In this chapter, you learn how to type a letter using AppleWorks, a suite of tools that includes a *word processor* (an application that specializes in text). You also learn incredibly useful iMac concepts like selecting, moving, cutting, copying, and pasting that you can use over and over again here and in other parts of your iMac. You discover how to "dress up" your text with fonts, styles, sizes, and colors. Finally, you learn how to save all your hard work!

Using AppleWorks

AppleWorks (which may also be called ClarisWorks on your iMac) can work minor miracles with your text. With it, you can do everything from write letters and jot notes to compose poetry and produce novels. It's much more than a glorified typewriter. You can even get fancy and create graphics, spreadsheets, and databases, but I get to that later. For now, use AppleWorks to write your first letter.

Opening AppleWorks

Begin by opening AppleWorks. You can find AppleWorks in your Applications folder on the Macintosh HD. The first time you open AppleWorks, you're asked for your name, your company's name, and/or your serial number or registration code. I assume you know your own name and company (or school or organization name).

However, the serial number may stump you. The AppleWorks serial number is the same as your iMac serial number, and you can find your iMac's serial number on your computer. Look for a label inside the access panel on the side of your iMac.

After you type your serial number, the New Document screen pops up so that you can create a new document. Just click OK and away you go!

Typing in AppleWorks

When a new document appears on your monitor, you should also see your text insertion point (the blinking vertical line in the upper-left corner). This is where your text appears as you type with your keyboard. You can begin typing as soon as this insertion point appears (see Figure 6-1).

Figure 6-1: Begin typing in your new AppleWorks document whenever you're ready.

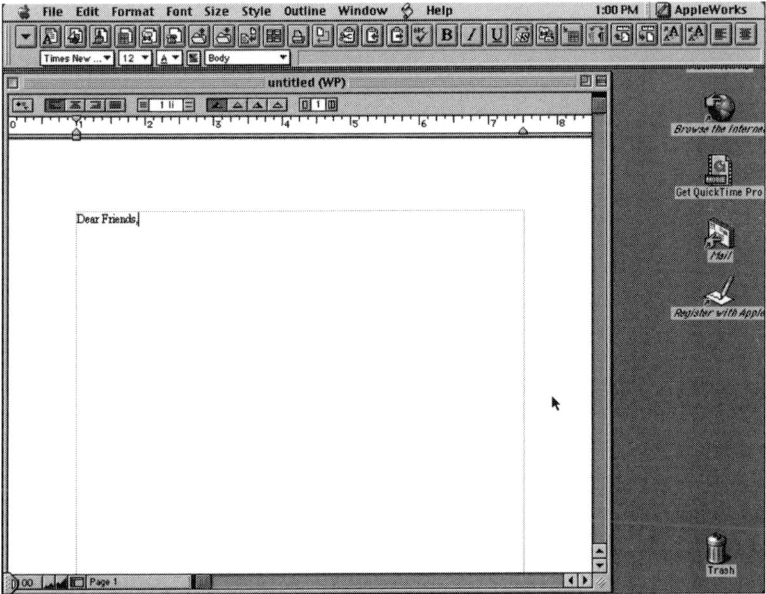

If you're used to a typewriter, you may be tempted to hit the Return key when you reach the right edge of your document. You don't need to do this on your iMac. Just keep typing and, when you get to the end of a line, your text "wraps" down to the next line automatically. This is called *word wrap*. You find word wrap in other applications on your iMac, too. You can (and should) use the Return key when you reach the end of a paragraph. You can also press Return when you want to force text to the next line for some reason.

Selecting and Moving Text

To prove that AppleWorks is more than a glorified typewriter, I'm going to show you how to select and move your text.

Before I can do that, though, you need to type some text. If you have a letter you've been meaning to write, this is the perfect time to start it. If you need a little hint, why not write a letter to me? I love to get mail and I really enjoy hearing what folks think of the iMac and my books. I even tell you how to send the letter directly to me at the end of the chapter.

After you have some text to work with, try some of these tricks:

- Position your pointer (which now looks like a capital *I*) over your text. Now click and drag to a new point — everything between your start and end point is *selected* (or *highlighted*). You can select a letter, set of letters, word, phrase, paragraph — as much text as you like.
- To select an entire word, position your pointer directly over the word and double-click.
- Triple-click (three quick clicks in a row) to select an entire line.
- Quadruple-click (four quick clicks) to select an entire paragraph (see Figure 6-2).

The text is now highlighted. In order to actually do something with your selected text, jump ahead to the next section.

After you master the art of selecting text, you may want to get back to typing your letter. To do this, just position your pointer at the end of your document (or wherever you want to add more text) and click once. Your insertion point moves to the location you clicked (or as close as possible). Your new text appears at the insertion point. This is called "drag-and-drop."

Figure 6-2: Your text becomes highlighted when you select it.

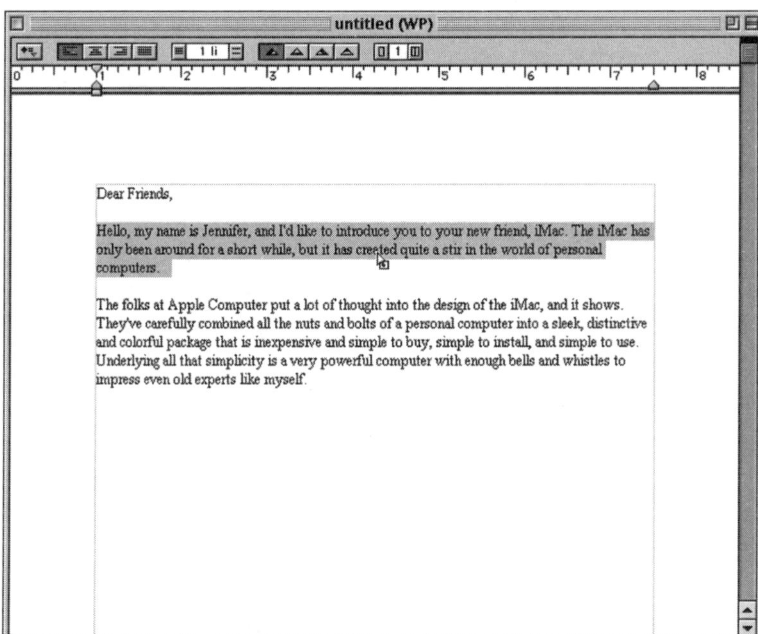

Cutting, Copying, and Pasting Text

Another incredibly useful set of features in AppleWorks and almost every other application on your iMac is the ability to cut, copy, and paste. No scissors, tape, or glue necessary! Here's the skinny on each feature:

- *Cut* means to remove text and hold on to it so that you can put it somewhere else.
- *Copy* means to save and hold text, but not remove it from its original position.
- *Paste* means to place the text you've cut or copied into your document.

Where does the text go when you cut or copy it? It goes to the *clipboard,* a special part of your iMac's memory specifically set aside to hold cut and copied items. You should know that the clipboard holds only one item at a time, which means that if you have something already on the clipboard and you cut or copy something else, the original contents of the clipboard disappear. So only the last item you cut or copy is actually on the clipboard.

Here's how to cut, copy, and paste text:

- **Cutting:** Select the text you'd like to cut. Now choose Edit⇨Cut or press ⌘+X. Your text disappears from the document and goes to the clipboard.
- **Copying:** Select the text you want to copy and choose Edit⇨Copy or press ⌘+C. You may not think anything happened, because the original text didn't disappear. But rest assured, a copy of the text now resides on the clipboard.
- **Pasting:** When you're ready to place the contents of the clipboard, position your pointer in the spot you want the text to appear and choose Edit⇨Paste or ⌘+V. Whatever text you placed on the clipboard immediately appears at your insertion point.

If nothing happens, the clipboard is probably empty. You can check the contents of the clipboard by choosing Edit⇨Show Clipboard. You can paste the same text over and over in different places — the text stays on the clipboard until you cut or copy something else, or restart your computer (see Figure 6-3).

Using Clear and Undo

You may be tempted to use the Cut command to remove text from a document, but a better way exists. Just select your text and choose Edit⇨Clear or press the Delete key. The text disappears. (And no, it doesn't go to the clipboard.)

Figure 6-3: You can paste over and over again if you want.

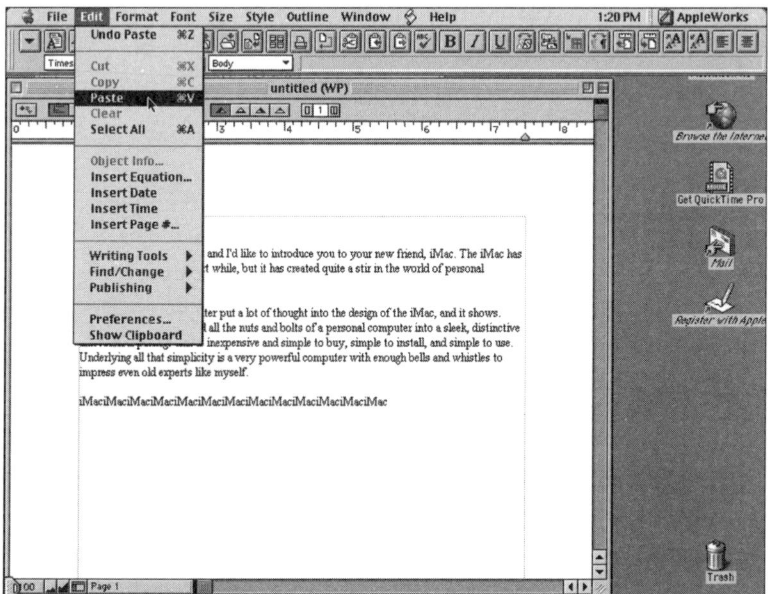

If you want to clear only one character of text at a time, here's how: Position your insertion point *at the end* (to the right) of the text you want to clear and press the Delete key. Each time you press Delete, you remove the character preceding the insertion point. Continue pressing Delete until all the text you want to delete is gone.

You can also hold down the Delete key to "mow" down all your letters very quickly. I don't recommend this method if you're deleting more than a few characters or words — the select-and-clear method is faster and more efficient.

Another way to clear text is to remove and replace it in one fell swoop! Just select the text you want to remove and use the Paste command — the original text disappears and the pasted text appears in its place. You can also select text and start typing for a similar effect.

Oops! Did you make a mistake? Don't worry — AppleWorks (and most other applications) enables you to back up a step and *undo*. Immediately choose Edit⇨Undo or press ⌘+Z. If you accidentally undo something (been there, done that), just revisit the Edit menu and choose Redo.

Applying Fonts and Styles

By now, you've noticed one of the nicer features of the iMac: What you see is what you get. When you type text, it appears on the screen as you go. When you delete text, it disappears right away. This feature is called *WYSIWYG* (pronounced "wizzywig," which stands for "What You See Is What You Get"). And you haven't seen anything yet! Your iMac can apply fonts and styles to your text, displaying them on your screen as they appear if you print the document.

Changing fonts

Fonts, also called *typefaces,* are electronic files that define a particular style of type in which you can display and print your text. Your iMac comes with about 40 fonts already installed and ready to use, and you're free to install lots more. To apply a new font to your text, select some or all the text, pull down the Fonts menu, and choose a font (see Figure 6-4).

Your text changes instantly! Don't like it? Choose another, or go back to the original font by pressing ⌘+Z.

If you find a font you really, really like, consider making it your default font for everything you type in AppleWorks. Just choose Edit⇨Preferences and select the font's name from the Default Font menu.

Figure 6-4: Changing your text font in AppleWorks is easy.

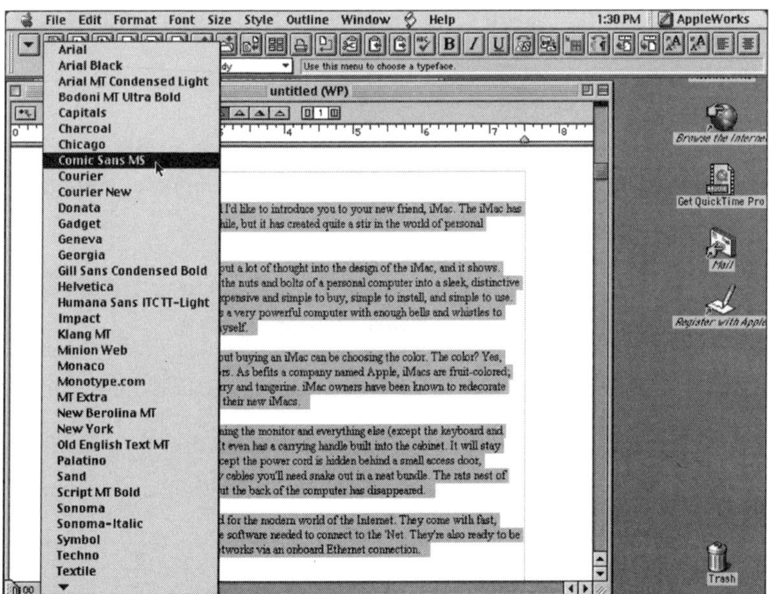

Changing sizes

Some fonts are so detailed that you can't read them without making them larger. To change text size, select the text you want to change, pull down the Size menu, and choose an appropriate size. The default size is usually 12, so if you want larger text, choose a higher number (and vice versa for smaller text). You can also use keyboard shortcuts to increase (Shift+⌘+>) or decrease (Shift+⌘+<) the size of your text, or choose another size altogether (Shift+⌘+O). Use the Other... command to choose a size lower than 9 and higher than 72, or any size in between that you don't see listed.

Changing styles

By default, all text you type is without style. No, that doesn't mean it doesn't look good, just that it has no extra formatting. You can apply styles, such as underlines, boldface, italics, and others when appropriate, however. Just select your text, pull down the Style menu, and choose an attribute.

Changing alignment

When the time comes for you to sign your name at the bottom of your letter, consider changing the text alignment so that your signature appears on the right side. To change text alignment, click one of the alignment buttons in the toolbar. (They look like sets of lines aligned in four different ways.) Here's what each alignment option does:

- **Left alignment** moves text flush against the left margin.
- **Center alignment** centers text in the middle of the page.
- **Right alignment** moves text flush against the right margin.
- **Justified alignment** makes all your lines the same width.

You can also change alignment by choosing Format⇨Paragraph.

Changing color

Add some color to your letter! Select your text and click the color button on the toolbar. (It looks like a prism of color.) Now choose a color from the grid. Use color sparingly, and keep in mind that only color printers can print colored text.

Saving Your Work

Time to save your work! Even if you haven't yet completed your letter, save it now.

In fact, I recommend saving your work as early and as often as possible. As I wrote this chapter, I must have saved it about 20 or 30 times. Saving a file is easy. Here's how:

1. Choose File⇨Save or press ⌘+S. A dialog box pops up and asks you to name your file and choose a location for it (see Figure 6-5).

Figure 6-5: Save your work early and often.

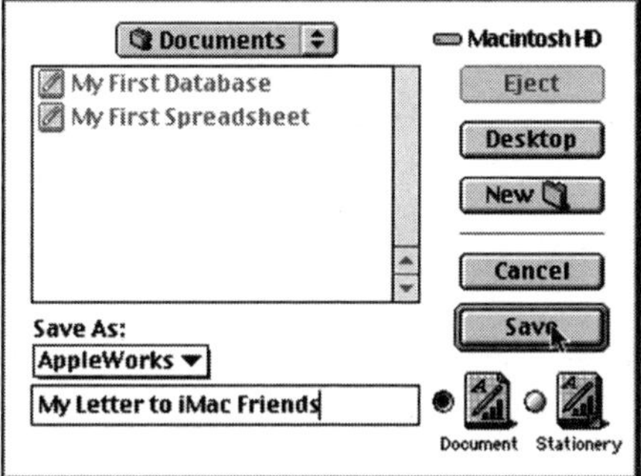

2. Click Save (or press Return) right away if you're in a hurry. Otherwise, type a name for your file, up to 31 characters long.

Your filename must be different from other filenames in the location you want to save it in. If you try to save something with the same name as another file in that location, you're asked if you want to replace the other file. Don't do that unless that's really your intention.

3. Choose a specific name, one that you can recognize and find later. Good spelling counts, too.

4. Use the drop-down menu at the top of the dialog box to navigate to a new location for your document, if you want to. You can go back to the desktop using either the drop-down menu or the desktop button on the right. You can also create a new folder to hold your document by clicking the New (Folder Icon) button.

5. Click Save or press the Return key.

CHAPTER 7

PRINTING YOUR FIRST LETTER

IN THIS CHAPTER

- Setting up a printer
- Using the Chooser
- Preparing to print
- Exercising your print options

Electronic files are great, but sometimes you just need a *hard copy*. Aunt Edna may not have a computer. Your club members may want extra copies to pass around. Or you may want to keep a permanent record in your files. Whatever the reason, printing is probably the solution.

Translating your computer data to paper requires a printer. The iMac by itself doesn't include a printer, though some of you may have bought an iMac package that included a printer. Or you may have purchased a printer separately, received one from a friend or family member, or used one you had before. However you got a printer, I can show you how to use it with your iMac. In this chapter, you learn to set up your printer, choose the right printer software, prepare your documents, and set your print options.

Setting Up a Printer

Setting up a printer involves two steps: physically connecting the printer to your iMac and installing the printer software. Before you begin, you should have the printer itself, plus any cables, software, and documentation that came with it. If you're missing any of these pieces, contact the source you got your printer from or phone the manufacturer.

Connecting your printer

The iMac uses the latest technology to connect peripherals like printers. It's called *Universal Serial Bus* (or USB for short). If your printer uses USB, you can connect it directly to your iMac — just plug its cable into one of the two USB ports behind your access door, or plug it into the spare USB port on your keyboard. For more info on USB, see Chapter 9. For now, I tell you only what you need to know to connect your printer.

If your printer doesn't have USB, check to see if it's Ethernet capable. If so, that works, too, though it is beyond the scope of this book to explain. If your printer uses something called AppleTalk (or LocalTalk), you need a special adapter to connect it to your printer. See the Resource Directory in the back of this book for more info.

In addition to the connection from the printer to the iMac, your printer needs power — plug its power cord into a wall outlet or surge suppressor. Now check your printer for any packing tape or material before you turn it on. Failure to remove them may cause serious problems. Read the documentation that came with your printer for any additional directions. After everything is set, power on your printer.

Installing your printer software

Most printers come with installation software for your iMac, usually on a CD-ROM. If your printer software came on floppy disks, contact the manufacturer for a CD-ROM (unless you purchased and installed a floppy disk drive). Install the printer software on your iMac according to the instructions, and then restart your iMac.

Using the Chooser

With your printer connected, your software installed, and your printer powered on, your next task is to tell your iMac which printer(s) you want to use. You must do this even if you only have one printer (go figure!). Follow these steps to do so:

1. Choose the Chooser from the Apple menu. The Chooser window opens (see Figure 7-1)

Figure 7-1: Use the Chooser to select a printer.

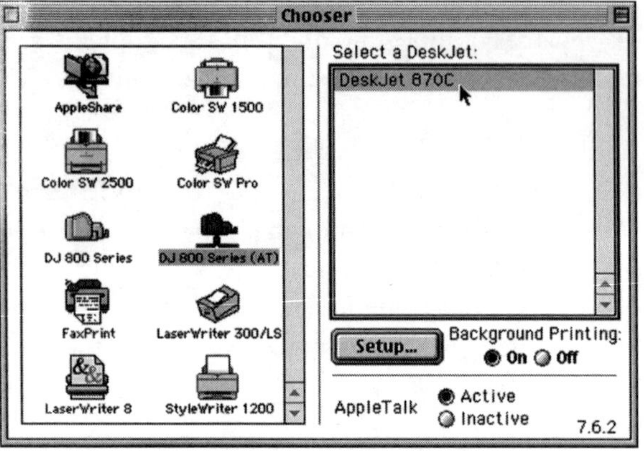

2. Locate and select your printer's icon in the box on the left. You should be able to recognize your printer by name — if you don't, check your printer's documentation or the installation software to see which icon to use. When you select the printer icon, the printer's name appears in the list on the right, indicating it is ready and waiting.
3. Click the printer name in the right box.
4. If everything went smoothly, close the Chooser window (click OK when prompted) and skip ahead to the next section. Otherwise, keep reading.

With so many different printers available, the chances that they all behave and work the same are impossible. Here are some tips for when you encounter difficulties:

- If you have a laser printer and don't see your laser printer's icon in the left box, try selecting the LaserWriter 8 icon instead. You should see your laser printer's name show up in the right box — click it and close the Chooser.
- If you do see your printer icon in the left box, but when you select it you see <Printer Port> and <Modem Port> appear in the right, that may be okay, too. If this happens, select <Printer Port> and then close the Chooser.
- If nothing shows up in the right box when you select your printer, make sure your printer is turned on; if not, try again. If that doesn't work, try turning your printer off and on again. (Your printer may need to warm up before it shows up in the Chooser, so wait a couple of minutes.) Also make sure that the AppleTalk radio button is enabled in the lower-right corner of the window.

After you select your printer in the Chooser, you probably won't have to revisit the Chooser. Unless you have more than one printer, in which case the Chooser becomes your best friend because you use the Chooser to change between printers.

Preparing to Print

In addition to setting up your printer, you also need to set up the document you want to print. Return to AppleWorks (choose it from the Application menu or just click one of the windows if it's visible in the background) and open your letter if you already closed it. Now follow these tried-and-true steps to prepare your document for printing:

1. Read (or scan) your document again.

   Is everything you wanted to include there? Are words spelled correctly? If you're not sure, pull down the Edit menu, display the Writing Tools menu, and select Check Document Spelling.

2. Check the page breaks.

   Do the pages break in the way you want? You can tell where a page breaks (where a new piece of paper will be needed when it is printed) by the thin, gray line. Don't like it? Change it by editing your text or choose Insert Page Break from the Format menu.

3. Check the margins.

   Are your margins large or small enough? Good margins are generally ¾ inch to 1 inch wide and should be no narrower than a half inch because your printer probably can't print that close to the edge of the paper. You can change your margins by choosing Format⇨Document.

4. Insert page numbers or footnotes at the bottoms of your pages, if you want. Choose Format⇨Document to set up page numbering and footnotes before you print.

5. If you're printing to a noncolor printer, change the colors to black to ensure they print out as crisp and clear as possible.

Using Page Setup

After your document is exactly the way you want it, choose File⇨Page Setup (see Figure 7-2).

The Page Setup window differs based on the type of printer you use, but some elements remain the same. Here's what each common option does:

Figure 7-2: One version of the Page Setup window. (Yours may look different.)

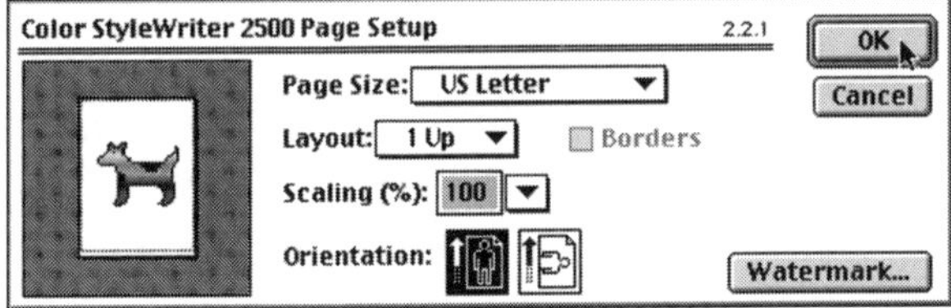

- The Page Size option enables you to select another paper size (such as legal size).
- The Layout option, if available, enables you to print several pages of a document onto one piece of paper, assuming your document is small enough.
- The Scale option allows you to increase or decrease the size of your document when it prints.
- The Orientation option determines whether your document is in the default portrait (vertical) or landscape (horizontal) view.

If you see a Utilities or Service button, click it to improve or maintain your printer.

Set your Page Setup options and click OK to save them.

Exercising Your Print Options

You're almost there! Only one task is left: telling your iMac how to print your document. Choose File➪Print, click the Printer icon on your toolbar, or just press ⌘+P.

As soon as you execute the Print command, a dialog box with print options pops up. (see Figure 7-3).

Figure 7-3: Set your print options before you print!

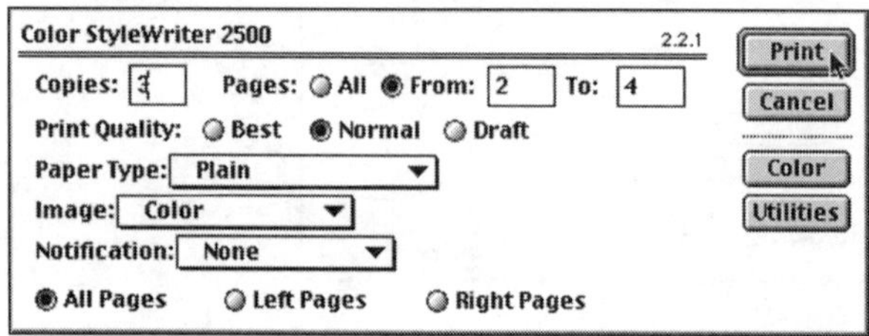

If you're not sure which settings to use, try the defaults. After you're ready, click Print (or just press Return). Your iMac sends the information to your printer and shows the printer's progress on the screen.

CHAPTER 8

SENDING YOUR FIRST FAX

IN THIS CHAPTER

- Using your fax software
- Creating a cover page
- Sending your fax
- Receiving a fax

Once upon a time, having "connections" meant knowing the *right* people. These days, you're just as likely to hear it used to describe someone with a street address, e-mail address, phone number, *and* fax number. And thanks to your iMac, you have all the right connections now, too!

Faxes are another alternative to e-mail, and your iMac does it just as well. Every iMac comes with fax software (called FAXstf) that you can use to send and receive faxes. In this chapter, you learn how to set up your fax software, create a cover page, send a fax, and receive a fax.

Using Your Fax Software

FAXstf does just one thing . . . but it does it well! It enables you to send and receive faxes directly from your iMac using your modem. Before you do anything else, make sure your telephone line cable is plugged into your iMac and a wall outlet (or a surge suppressor, which also needs to be plugged into a wall outlet).

Configuring FAXstf

Start by opening the FAXstf application, called Fax Browser — you can find it in your Applications folder. The first time you open FAXstf, you get the option to register now or later. Registration is always a good idea, but you can register later if you prefer. The Fax Browser window appears on your screen after the application is up and running.

Your first task is to configure your fax software for your purposes. Here's how:

1. Choose Edit⇨Settings; in the resulting window, you see a line of icons along the left side, each representing a different group of settings.
2. In the Cover Page settings, type your name, company/school/organization name, voice (telephone) number, and fax number (if it is different from your voice number).

   The remaining settings are probably acceptable as they are, though you may want to visit each one and tweak the settings as necessary. Pay particular attention to the Fax Menu settings — the check boxes here indicate which keys you should press and hold when you want to fax something without using the Chooser. I explain how that works later, but for now, note (or change) the activation key(s).
3. Close your settings when you finish.

Setting up your phone book

FAXstf lets you store phone numbers in the software, which I recommend you set up in advance whenever possible. To add a phone number, follow these steps:

1. Choose Windows⇨Fax Numbers (or click the Phonebook button in the Fax Browser window).

2. Before making any changes, unlock the phonebook — just click the Unlock Phonebook button.
3. Choose Action➪New Contact (or click the New Contact button) for a blank line in the chart below.
4. Type in all relevant information (be sure to include at least a name and a fax number).
5. Repeat Steps 3 and 4 to add more contacts.
6. When finished, click Lock Phonebook again to protect your data.

You may notice a lot of other buttons and commands in the Fax Browser, but most of them are just extras. I touch on them later in this chapter when they make more sense. For now, I discuss the Cover Page feature!

Creating a Cover Page

What's a good fax without a cover page? Like any good fax application, FAXstf lets you create and send cover pages. Better yet, FAXstf enables you to predefine up to ten different cover pages that you can use quickly and easily. This is where having fax software on your computer really comes in handy!

Follow these steps to create a cover page:

1. Choose Edit➪Edit Cover Pages; the resulting window offers a variety of options and an image of what your cover page will look like (see Figure 8-1).
2. Choose Empty Cover Page from the drop-down menu.
3. Give your new cover page a title and indicate its size (half or full page).
4. Click Edit Labels Text to change the label font and any of the labels themselves. I recommend you keep the

Figure 8-1: Creating a new cover page is easy.

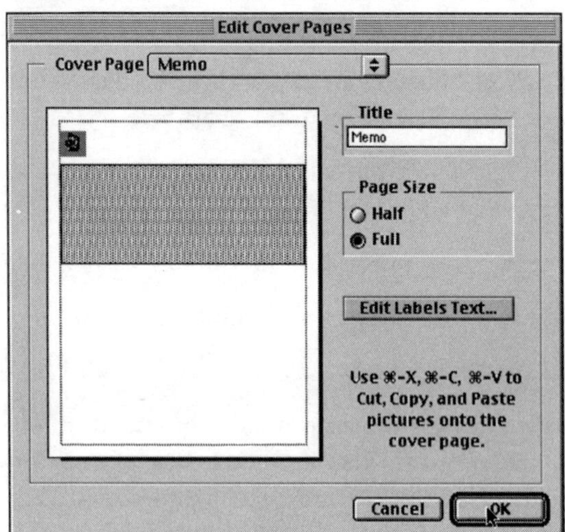

labels just the way they are, unless you have something specific in mind. The information you entered into your Cover Page settings appears here when you send a fax.

5. Click Cancel to leave the labels unchanged or OK to save any modifications.

6. When you're ready, click OK to save your new cover page. You can later return here to edit the cover page or create a new one.

Sending Your Fax

FAXstf provides two simple ways to send your faxes. If your note is short and you want to dash if off, you can use the QuickNote feature to send a fax up to 255 characters in size. Most of the time, you may find that sending your fax directly from another application, such as AppleWorks, is just as easy.

Faxing with QuickNote

To send a simple note via fax, follow these steps:

1. Choose File⇨Send a QuickNote (or press ⌘+K).
2. Type in your recipient's contact information (or click and drag the recipient's entry from your phonebook).
3. Type your note in the Cover Page Note box.
4. Choose a cover page from the drop-down menu, if you wish.
5. When you're ready, click Send Fax. The FAXstf application immediately sends the fax to your recipient, keeping you up-to-date on its progress as it goes. If you need to cancel the fax, just click Stop.

If the phone number is busy or there is no answer, the fax goes into the Fax Hold folder in your Fax Browser. FAXstf retries the number again. (Check your Fax Software settings to change the number of retries and interval between them.)

Faxing from an application

To send a document from another application, follow these steps:

1. Open that application and the document you want to fax.
2. Open your Chooser (from the Apple menu), select the FaxPrint icon, close the Chooser, and choose Fax from the File menu.

   An even easier way is to forego the Chooser altogether and hold down those activation key(s) I mentioned earlier (defaults are Option+⌘) while displaying the File menu. You should see Fax at the bottom of the File menu!

   Either way you do it, you get the FaxPrint window (see Figure 8-2).

Figure 8-2: Address your fax in the FaxPrint window.

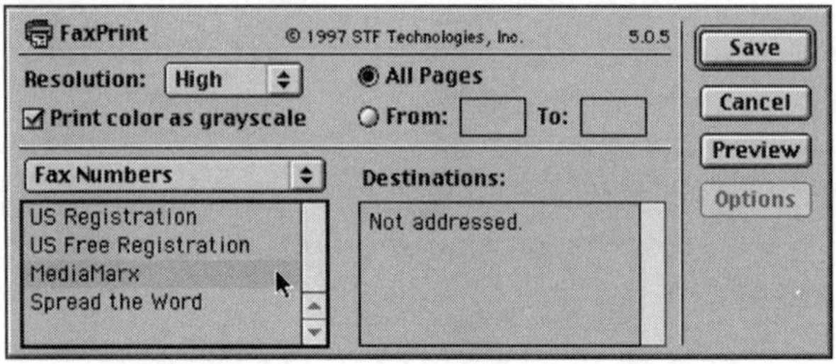

The FaxPrint window bears some resemblance to the Print Options window. You can specify Resolution (choose High for the best quality or Low for fastest transmission speed). You can choose to print all pages in your document or specify a range of pages. You also have the option of "printing" (converting) colors in your document to grayscale — disable it if you want all colors to show up as black in your fax.

The FaxPrint window is also where you decide whom your fax goes to. You should see all the contacts you added to your phonebook in the list on the left — if you don't, select Fax Numbers from the drop-down menu. (If you still don't see your contacts, return to the Fax Browser and close your Phonebook — it needs to be closed to send its data to the FaxPrint window.)

3. To address your fax, double-click one of the contact names in the list.
4. Click Address in the resulting window to add it to your Destinations list on the right side. You can have more than one destination, too! Just keep double-clicking contacts or select a name and press ⌘+]. If you want to address a fax to a name that isn't in your phonebook, select Temporary Address from the drop-down menu on the left of your fax window and enter the contact information.
5. Click the Options button on the right side to schedule your fax for later or to choose a cover page. After you

choose a cover page, you can also type a note that will be sent within your cover page. Click OK to save your options.

6. Click Send to transmit your fax. If you scheduled it for later, your fax is placed in the Fax Out folder within FAXstf until the time comes to send it. Otherwise, your iMac immediately transmits the fax to your recipient(s).

Receiving a Fax

FAXstf can receive faxes automatically, but you need to configure it to do so first. Here's how:

1. Revisit your Settings (under the Edit menu) and click the Fax Modem icon.
2. From the Answer-On drop-down menu, select on which ring your iMac answers the fax.

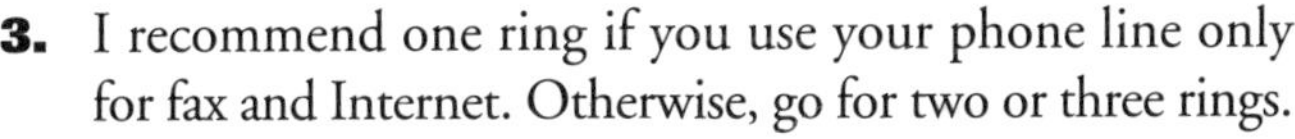

3. I recommend one ring if you use your phone line only for fax and Internet. Otherwise, go for two or three rings.

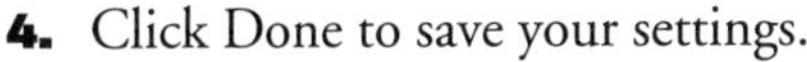

4. Click Done to save your settings.

Now when your phone rings, your iMac automatically answers it after the number of rings you indicated in your settings. If the call is a fax, your iMac receives it for you and displays a fax progress.

I recommend that you either use FAXstf only on a dedicated modem line or turn off the automatic answer feature when you're not expecting a fax.

After successfully receiving the fax, you hear a "ringing phone" sound and a blinking icon appears over the Apple menu to indicate you have a new fax. Go to your Fax Browser, click Fax In, and double-click your fax to view it.

CHAPTER 9
USING DISKS AND SCANNERS

IN THIS CHAPTER

- Understanding the Universal Serial Bus (USB)
- Mastering hard drives
- Making the most of your CD-ROM drive
- Using removable media drives
- Working with scanners and digital cameras
- Using other peripherals

Universal Serial Bus (or USB) is the hot, new technology built into your iMac. I could get technical here, but it really isn't necessary. USB is very simple to use. But what does it do, you wonder? USB takes the place of all the miscellaneous jacks and ports the Mac used to sport, like modem jacks, printer jacks, ADB ports, SCSI connectors, and more. With all those jacks and ports came all sorts of pesky details about what went where and how it all worked. Those days are over. Your iMac has four USB jacks into which you can connect four USB devices — be they keyboards, mice, joysticks, printers, drives, speakers, scanners, or digital cameras.

Of your four USB jacks, two are located on your keyboard and two behind your iMac's access panel. Thus two of those four are in use already — your mouse is connected to one jack on your keyboard and your keyboard is connected to one jack behind your access panel. If you have a printer, it may be connected to a third jack. If you plan to have more than four USB devices connected to your iMac, you can buy an adapter box and add up to 127 more USB devices to your iMac. Can you even imagine?

The only real catch to all this is that when you purchase gadgets like hard drives, floppy disk drives, scanner, cameras, and so on, they need to work with USB. Don't just assume something works — check specifically to see if it is a USB device. You shouldn't have to look too hard, however. More and more Mac equipment comes USB-ready. If you have an older device that doesn't use USB, you can still use it if you buy a USB adapter to translate the data. See the Resource Center for details.

Armed with this information, you can now successfully choose, purchase, and install USB gadgets. In this chapter, I take a look at the different kinds of toys you can get or may already have for your iMac!

Mastering Hard Drives

A *hard drive* (also called a *hard disk*) is the storage area of your iMac. Massive amounts of information can be recorded (written) on and retrieved (read) from the hard drive. You already have one hard drive, which is safely concealed inside your iMac. You've been accessing your hard drive all along through the Macintosh HD icon on your desktop. In fact, your hard drive holds the Mac OS, without which your iMac would be a colorful doorstop. When you install programs onto your computer, the hard drive is where they reside. All the documents you save also go to the hard drive.

Should you want to expand your storage capacity, you can purchase and connect another hard drive, though you may need to also purchase an adapter for it because not many hard drives come USB-ready as yet. Deciding what size hard drive to get is the key. The hard drive inside your iMac is probably either 4 or 6GB. If you're not sure, go to your desktop, select your Macintosh HD icon, and press ⌘+I. The resulting window gives your hard drive's capacity (see Figure 9-1). Whether your capacity is 4 or 6GB, that's usually more than enough for most folks.

Figure 9-1: The Info window shows your hard drive capacity (among other things).

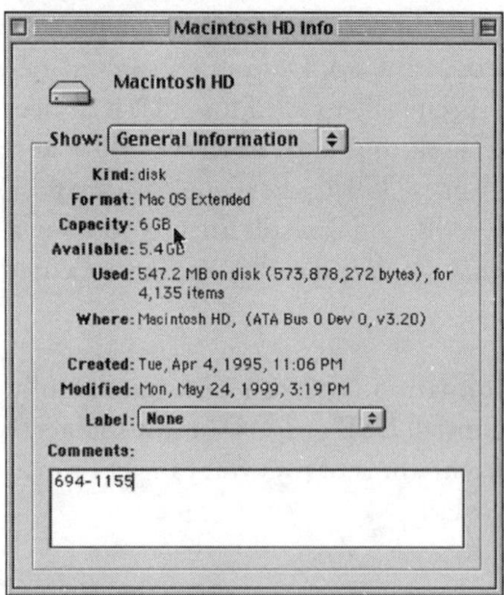

If you're not sure what GB (let alone MB or K) means, here's a quick primer on storage units:

- A kilobyte is 1,024 bytes. A typical document is between 10 and 100K. (K is short for kilobytes and is pronounced "kay.") For example, you can say, "The iMac Read Me document is 24K."
- A megabyte is 1,024K. A typical application program is between 5 and 50MB. (MB is short for megabytes.) Usually folks shorten megabytes to "meg" or "megs" when speaking about them. For example, you'd say, "AppleWorks is about 30 megs."
- A gigabyte is 1,024MB. (GB is short for gigabytes.) Most people shorten gigabytes to "gig" or "gigs" when referring to them. For example, you can say, "My iMac has a 6-gig hard drive."

Making the Most of Your CD-ROM Drive

In addition to your hard drive, your iMac comes with a built-in CD-ROM drive. A CD-ROM drive differs from a hard drive in two important ways:

- You can only *read* (retrieve) information from a CD-ROM drive. You cannot write (record) information using your iMac's CD-ROM drive.
- You need to insert a CD-ROM disc to use the drive. CD-ROM drives are pretty useless without something to put in them.

Your iMac comes with a folder of CD-ROM *discs* — some are for your Mac OS software; others are for various programs bundled with your iMac. You can read the discs with your iMac's built-in CD-ROM reader. Here's how:

1. Open the CD-ROM tray by pushing the oblong button directly below the word *iMac* on the front of your computer. The tray pops out for you, but not all the way. Gently pull the tray toward you until it stops. If the tray doesn't pop out for some reason, you may already have a CD-ROM disc in your iMac — if so, keep reading to learn how to eject it.
2. Take a CD-ROM disc from its sleeve or case. Be careful not to touch the underside of the disc, because oil and dust can easily confuse the CD-ROM reader. Hold it only by the edges and place it in the tray label up and shiny side down.
3. Press the center down until it snaps onto the spindle.
4. Gently push the tray back into your computer until it clicks into place. The CD-ROM disc spins up and you hear a whirring noise, then an icon representing your CD-ROM disc appears on your desktop.

5. If a window for the disc doesn't open, just double-click the disc icon. Now all the data on the CD-ROM is available to read, run, install, and so on — just double-click the appropriate items in the disc window like you would anything else on your desktop.

When you finish using a CD-ROM disc, eject it and put it away. Here's how:

1. First, close all open windows, files, and programs you may have opened.
2. Drag the disc icon on top of the trash icon. Don't worry — this won't remove any data from the disc. Alternately, select the disc icon and choose Special⇨Eject, or File⇨Put Away. Your CD-ROM tray pops open again and you can remove the disc.
3. Put the disc back in its sleeve or case for protection and close the tray.

Oh, and just in case it wasn't obvious, CD-ROM drives also play audio CDs. Put one in and try it out!

You may have heard of CDs that you can *write to* as well as *read from*. These are called CD-Rs (the R stands for *recordable*) or CD-RWs (which let you record, erase, and record again). If this interests you, you can purchase a CD-R or CD-RW drive and connect it to your iMac.

Using Removable Media Drives

Removable media drive is a fancy term for things like CD-ROM drives, SuperDisk drives, and Zip drives. You found out about CD-ROM drives in the previous section, but what about the others? Essentially, they are storage devices with portable disks. The disks are usually small and inexpensive. So if you need more storage space, you buy more disks.

Some people use them to transfer data from one computer to another, and some people use them to *back up* (archive) their data just in case anything happens to it. If you decide that a removable media drive may be useful, you can purchase and connect one to your iMac if the drive is USB-ready.

To use a removable media disk, insert it into its drive slot — metal side first and label side up. Push the disk in until it clicks or becomes flush with the slot. If your disk already contains data, its icon appears on your desktop much like a CD-ROM disc. Double-click it and off you go! If the disk is brand new, your iMac may ask you if you want to initialize it (see Figure 9-2).

Figure 9-2: You may need to initialize disks.

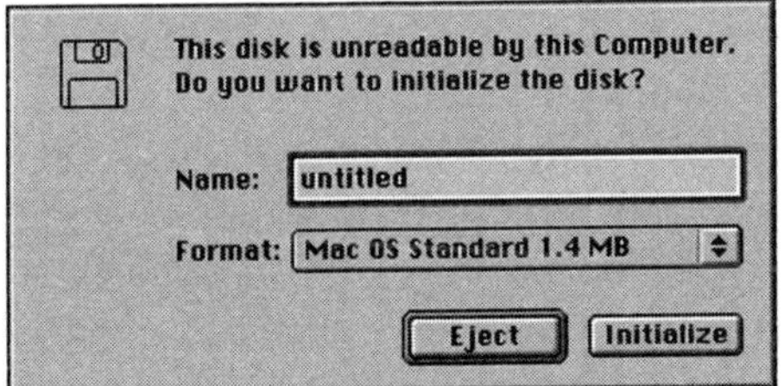

Go ahead and click Initialize if the disk really is brand new — otherwise, eject it and take it back to the source because the disk may be damaged.

Keep in mind that whenever you initialize a disk, all the data on the disk is destroyed. So be careful and make sure you really want to initialize before you do.

Like CD-ROM discs, you need to protect your removable media disks. Store them in their cases or sleeves and keep them away from magnets and dust. You don't need to be as careful about how you hold the disk — the plastic case protects it better.

Working with Scanners and Digital Cameras

Whether you're a graphic artist or the family picture-taker, scanners and digital cameras can be fun and useful. These two devices are similar, but you use them in different ways. You can use a *scanner* to record images of photos you've taken, artwork you've made, or pretty much anything else that's flat — then store the images on your hard disk. *Digital cameras* record images more like traditional cameras, only the images are digital rather than imposed on film. Both open up new possibilities for taking and sharing pictures. You can purchase a USB-ready scanner and/or digital camera for your iMac, too!

Even if you're not into pictures, you may be interested in a scanner for its OCR capabilities. *OCR* stands for *optical character recognition*, which means it can scan a document, translate it to text, and save it in a file for you. You're then free to edit the text in any way you like. This can be a real timesaver!

You can also edit the graphic files created by scanners and digital cameras. In fact, your iMac comes with software that lets you do just that! I show you how that works in the next chapter.

Using Other Peripherals

The iMac has a lot of toys. Call them peripherals, or devices, or equipment if you like — but I think toys is a much more accurate description (and more fun!). Some of them even come styled in the translucent plastic like your iMac.

If you'd like to learn about more toys, particularly the latest and greatest ones, visit `www.macintouch.com/imacusb.html` on the Internet.

CHAPTER 10

MAKING AND MODIFYING GRAPHICS

IN THIS CHAPTER

- Using the drawing tools
- Using the painting tools
- Modifying a photo
- Understanding graphic file formats

In the unlikely event that you haven't noticed, your iMac is very graphics-oriented. If the icons didn't give it away, your software will! Bundled with your iMac are several graphic applications that let you create and edit in a variety of graphic formats. You can paint with brushes, draw with pens, touch up photos, and make all sorts of changes.

You may feel inclined to skip over this chapter if you're not artistically inclined, but I encourage you to stay and read anyway. You can learn valuable skills that translate to other programs — and have a lot of fun in the process. Besides, you may be surprised at how your iMac can bring out the artist in you!

Using the Drawing Tools

AppleWorks offers a drawing program in addition to its word processing capabilities. Here's how to get started:

- Open AppleWorks and select Drawing from the list before you click OK.
- With AppleWorks already open, click the toolbar icon that has a triangle, circle, and square on it.

Either way, AppleWorks opens a new drawing document (see Figure 10-1).

Figure 10-1: A new canvas for drawing in AppleWorks.

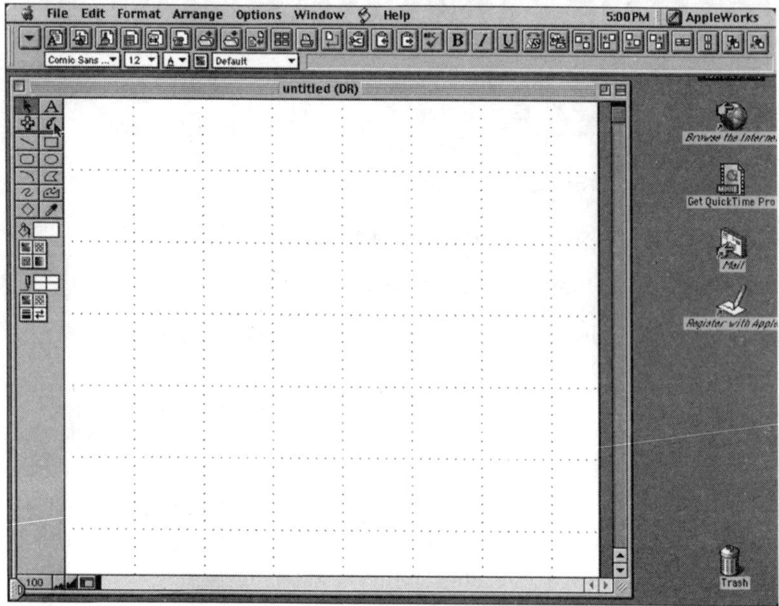

Along the left side of the window is the drawing tool palette. The majority of the window is your *canvas* (the place you draw on). Try it out now by selecting the oval tool from the palette, and then click and drag your mouse across the canvas. An oval appears, along with four black squares around it. These black squares are your *handles* — click and drag one to change the shape of your oval. These handles are always available to resize something on the canvas — if you don't see them, click once on the object to show them again.

You can do only so much with the oval tool, of course. Try out the other tools by selecting them one at a time from the palette and dragging them across the canvas. Most of the tools are self-explanatory, but if you aren't sure what something does, try this trick:

1. Choose Help⇨Show Balloons and move your pointer over one of the tools on your palette (but don't click it). A help balloon pops up to explain what the tool does.
2. When you're done with the balloons, hide them again by choosing File⇨Hide Balloons.

After you draw a shape, you can fill it with colors, patterns or textures — even change the thickness of its border. Just select the object you want to modify, and then choose something from the two button quadrants at the bottom of your tool palette. The top quadrant fills the object with a color, pattern, texture, or gradient. The bottom quadrant changes the border color, pattern, and width. (The bottom-right button in the lower quadrant applies arrows to straight lines.)

If you draw something you don't like, you can get rid of it in two ways. If you just drew it, choose Edit⇨Undo. Otherwise, select it (so you can see its handles) and press Delete on your keyboard.

Using the Painting Tools

Painting is a far different beast than drawing. Drawing works with objects, whereas painting works with pixels. What are *pixels?* Get up close to your monitor and look at it — do you see the tiny dots that compose text and images? Those are pixels. Don't worry — you don't have to paint one pixel at a time. But you could if you wanted. Painting is more challenging but also affords more control.

If you still have your drawing on your screen in AppleWorks, click the icon of a paintbrush on the toolbar to create a new painting document. If you closed AppleWorks, open it and select Painting in the list when prompted to create a new document. A blank painting document window appears on the screen — again, your tool palette is on the left and your canvas takes up the rest of the window.

If you tried your hand at drawing in the previous section, the painting window should look familiar to you. You may notice a few additional tools you didn't have before, however. Here they are:

- Three tools (selection rectangle, lasso, and magic brush) let you select groups of pixels — remember, you're no longer working with objects that have handles.
- You also have a brush (to "paint" with), a pencil (to "sketch" with), a paint bucket (to fill an area), and a spray can (to "scatter" paint).
- Most importantly, you now have an eraser tool to remove parts of your painting, if you want.

Click the paintbrush tool, and then click and drag it across the canvas. You can change the width of your brush by double-clicking the paintbrush tool, selecting a new brush size (and/or shape), and clicking OK. Experiment with other tools, colors, patterns, textures, gradients, and so on. Unlike drawings, however, you must choose your colors, patterns, and so on before you paint. Choosing a color or pattern afterward only affects the next thing you paint, not the last thing (see Figure 10-2).

If you make a mistake, choose File⇨Undo. If that doesn't help, click the Eraser tool, and click and drag over the mistake in your painting. If you want to erase your entire painting, double-click the eraser tool.

I can't cover all the tools or techniques in this brief chapter, but I recommend you spend some time with AppleWorks and have fun! You'll probably learn a lot more that way than reading about it.

If you want to learn more about painting (and drawing), choose AppleWorks Help Index from the Help menu.

Figure 10-2: My iMac . . . isn't she cute?

Modifying a Photo

Another cool thing you can do on the iMac is modify a photo. It can be a photo you snapped with a digital camera, scanned with a scanner, or simply found on the Internet. It does need to be on your iMac in digital form, however (by digital form I mean that it should be in a graphic file format on your hard drive).

Before you can modify your photo, you need to install one of the bundled applications that came with your iMac: Kai's Photo Soap. The CD-ROM is in the CD case that came with your iMac. Here's what you do:

1. Insert the CD-ROM into the CD-ROM tray.
2. Double-click the disc's icon on your desktop to open its window.

3. Double-click on the icon labeled English.
4. Double-click the Kai's Photo Soap SE Installer icon.
5. Click Continue, and click Continue again.
6. Choose a location for the application from the Install Location drop-down menu.
7. Click the paintbrush to install the software.
8. Restart your iMac.

After your iMac has restarted, open Kai's Photo Soap. You can tell immediately upon opening that this is an artistic sort of application. Don't be put off by how different everything looks — you can still click buttons and select things like you do everywhere else on your iMac.

Photo file ready to modify? Click File on the left side to locate and open your photo. (If you don't have a photo file, experiment with one of the photos in the Images folder inside Kai's Photo Soap folder.) The photo opens on your screen, ready for you to modify (see Figure 10-3).

Kai's Photo Soap really excels at enhancement! You can brighten faded photos, you can sharpen old black and whites, and you can eliminate those infamous "red eyes." You need to move to different parts of the *studio* to do different things to your photo — just click Map at the top of your screen and choose a room. Here's what you can do in each room:

- **In Room:** This is where you entered Kai's Photo Soap. Open files and folders of files, save "albums," preview photos, and more.
- **Prep Room:** This is where your photo appears after opening it. You can resize, rotate, and crop your photo here.
- **Tone Room:** Here, you adjust the tonal balance of your photo, including intensity, brightness, and contrast.

Figure 10-3: A photo ready to be prepped in Kai's Photo Soap.

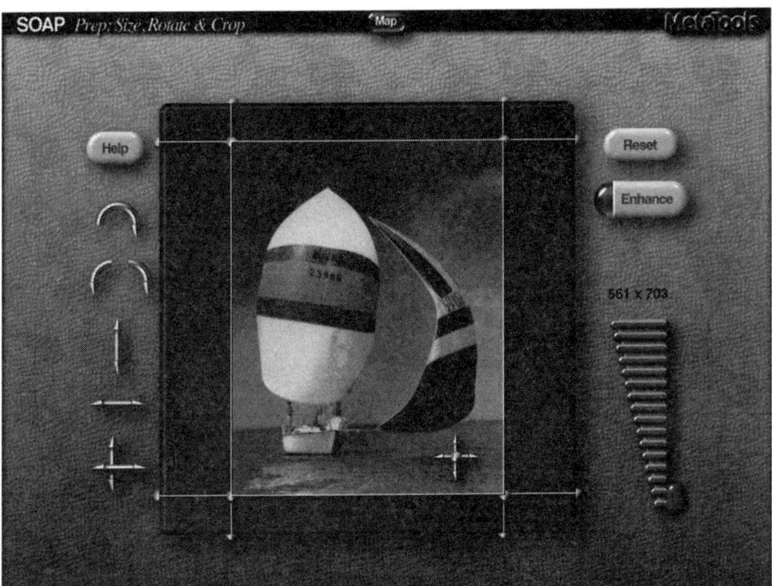

- **Color Room:** This is where you can change your photo's hue, saturation, and color brightness.
- **Detail Room:** Sharpen and smooth photos, plus remove red eye, clean up dust and scratches, and clone parts of your picture.
- **Finish Room:** In this room, you can add text, backgrounds, photo edges, and clip art, plus flip and rotate your photo.
- **Out Room:** Here's where you save and/or print your photo and select a resolution (quality level).

Understanding Graphic File Formats

Both AppleWorks and Kai's Photo Soap can save the images and photos you work on. Yet, the first time you go to save a graphic, you may be stumped by all the choices: JPEG, PICT, PSD, TIFF, BMP, Flash Pix, and GIF are all options. Here is a quick list of these acronyms, their meanings, and my comments about the usefulness of each format:

- **BMP:** This is the Windows native graphic format. Use this if you plan to give a graphic to someone using Windows.
- **FPX:** This stands for Flash Pix, a new graphic format that offers advanced resolution. Use it if an application (or person) asks for it.
- **GIF:** A popular graphic format on the Internet. Quality is not high, however. Use this to exchange files, particularly simple line art, across the Internet.
- **JPEG:** Both AppleWorks and Kai's Photo Soap support it, so do other applications on your iMac. JPEG isn't the best quality. Use JPEG to send photos over the Internet.
- **PICT:** Your iMac's native graphic format. It isn't used by many other applications or computer systems. PICT files can be large.
- **PSD:** This is the format of a popular graphics application, Adobe PhotoShop. Use this format only with PhotoShop.
- **TIFF:** This is a high-quality image format that is also compressed. Use this if you plan to reproduce your images on a printing press.

CHAPTER 11

MOVING FORWARD WITH YOUR IMAC

IN THIS CHAPTER

- Learning from the Help menu
- Solving problems and conflicts
- Playing, accounting, and cooking
- Mastering everyday skills

You deserve a hand for making it to the end of the book. And this chapter is your reward. It's full of tips and tricks on making the most of your iMac and moving ahead with it. You discover how to learn more about your iMac, solve those pesky problems and conflicts, and use a few more of your bundled applications. Finally, I leave you with some everyday skills you may find helpful throughout your career on the iMac.

Learning from the Help Menu

Sometimes the best thing to do is just call for Help! And your iMac offers some of the most comprehensive help resources available — all within easy reach in the Help menu. You could wait until you needed help to visit it, or you could become acquainted with the resources available now. If you have the time, go for the latter. You'd be surprised how much it can help you when you really *do* need the help!

Help Center

The first item in your Help menu (when you're in the Finder) is the Help Center (see Figure 11-1).

Figure 11-1: The Help Center stands ready to lend a hand.

You can search for help on a specific term, or better yet, click one of the hyperlinks for topic-by-topic information. I particularly recommend the About Your iMac section, which offers tips on saving energy, using headphones and a microphone, connecting to a network, installing more memory (RAM), avoiding fatigue, handling your iMac, and staying secure. The Mac OS Help section explains all the nitty-gritty details of your operating system, including disks, files, memory, monitors, printing, sound, speech, and much more! You can also reach Mac OS Help by pressing the ⌘+? keys. Both of these sections are excellent supplements to this book when you want to learn more.

Balloon Help

Balloon Help works best when you're not sure what something on your screen does. Just turn on your Balloon Help (choose Help➪Show Balloons) and move your pointer over the area. A balloon offers information and/or tips (see Figure 11-2). To disable Balloon Help, just choose Help➪Hide Balloons.

Figure 11-2: Balloon help can solve many riddles.

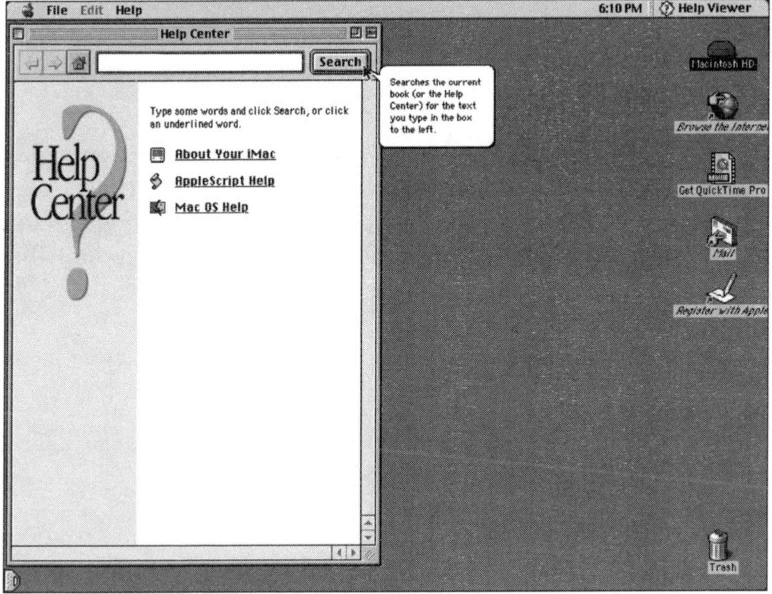

Tutorial

The Mac OS Tutorial is a step-by-step, animated tour of your iMac. It focuses on two essential skills: using the mouse and using the desktop. I highly recommend it, even if you're a master at both. Its fun, entertaining, and quintessentially Mac. Let me know if you find the secret tomb!

Solving Problems and Conflicts

It's inevitable — you *will* encounter problems. While, in my opinion, iMacs have fewer problems than other computers, they aren't without their pesky points. One thing you don't need to do is "live" with a problem, however. All problems have solutions. I can't cover everything here, but I try to hit the major issues you may encounter.

If you stumble across a problem that I don't cover here, check the Resource Center at the back of this book for more books on using your Mac, or call Apple's tech support number.

Thawing freezes

Sometimes, your iMac just freezes. Everything stops, your mouse may or may not work, but you can't do anything. Your goal is to get things moving again, preferably without restarting your iMac (though that is often the only solution). Try these things, in this order:

- Wait a few seconds (or a few minutes). Sometimes your iMac is just thinking really hard.
- Press ⌘+(period) to Cancel the action that preceded the freeze.
- Press ⌘+Q to Quit the application that's frozen. If your iMac asks if you want to save your work, do so.
- Press ⌘+Option+Esc to force a quit. You see a dialog box asking if you really want to force quit the application or cancel the force quit.

When you force quit a particular application, you lose any changes you made since the last save. So be sure that you really want to force quit.

- Press Control+Option+Power Button on your keyboard. This action restarts your iMac without quitting the open applications. Any unsaved work is lost.
- Use the Restart button: Push a straightened paper clip into the teeny-weeny hole between your phone jack and your USB ports in your access panel.

If one of the first four options works, immediately save any work you have open in other applications and restart your iMac. If the fifth and sixth options don't work (they should restart your iMac for you), you may have to pull the iMac power cord out of the outlet — this should definitely be your last resort, however.

Resolving conflicts

If your iMac freezes a lot, especially when you first start it up, you may have a conflict between some of the software in your iMac.

The key to identifying your conflicts lies with your Extension Manager (under the Apple menu in your Control Panels). If your iMac freezes on start up, restart it using one of the techniques in the preceding section and hold down the space bar during startup. The Extension Manager window appears. Start by disabling everything. Now the trick is to re-enable each item in the Extension Manager until you find the one item that is causing the conflict. This can take a *lot* of time — and a lot of restarts.

If you don't have the time and patience to go through this process, you can purchase an application called Conflict Catcher, which, as you may have guessed, identifies conflicts. You can get more information and a free trial at `www.casadyg.com`.

Allocating more memory

Another source of freezes may be applications without enough memory. They may be polite about it and *tell* you they're out of memory, or they may just freeze. Here's how to allocate more memory to an application:

1. Quit the application, if it's open.
2. Select the application's icon (not its folder) on your desktop.

3. Press ⌘+I. The Get Info window appears.
4. Choose Memory from the drop-down Show menu (see Figure 11-3).

Figure 11-3: You can change an application's memory allocation.

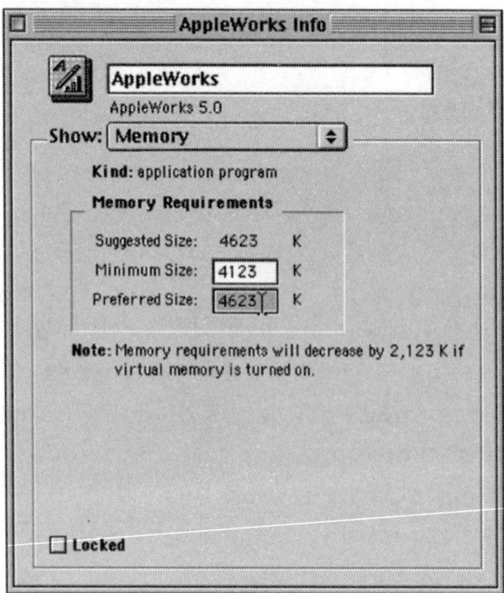

5. Type a new number in the Preferred Size box — it should be higher than the suggested or minimum size (but probably not more than double).
6. Close the box and reopen your application.

Playing, Accounting, and Cooking

Your iMac comes with several additional applications that you should find entertaining and educational. Some are already installed on your hard drive (check your Applications folder), while others need to be installed from CD-ROM discs in your iMac box. Here's a run-down on what they are.

Nanosaur

Nanosaur is a shoot-'em-up, dinosaur game and a real blast! After opening the application, keep hitting the spacebar until you get to the screen with the nanosaur and the falling, blue-speckled eggs, and then hit the Return key to begin playing. Alternately, you can press the right or left arrow keys to cycle through the various options: Play (nanosaur), High Scores, Exit, Help (question mark), and Options (check mark). The object of the game is to collect five different dinosaur eggs and transport them back to the future before the giant asteroid hits and destroys all life on Earth. Use the arrow keys to move your nanosaur left, right, and forward to hunt for the eggs. If you see any dinosaurs come at you, press the spacebar to shoot 'em!

Quicken Deluxe

Quicken Deluxe (see Figure 11-4) is a personal finance manager that helps you keep track of bank accounts, cash transactions, assets and liabilities, credit card balances, stock portfolios, and mutual funds. You can write checks with Quicken, automatically balance your checkbook with each check, and then print out the checks on your printer. You can also set up Quicken to pay your bills electronically through the Internet.

Williams-Sonoma Guide to Good Cooking

Williams-Sonoma Guide to Good Cooking has recipes, recipes, and more recipes — all illustrated and searchable. My favorite feature is the ability to enter the ingredients you have in the kitchen and get a list of dishes you can make with them.

If you have file sharing enabled, be sure to disable it before you install or run this application — otherwise your computer will crash (been there, done that).

Figure 11-4: Insert your CD-ROM to play Quicken's tutorials.

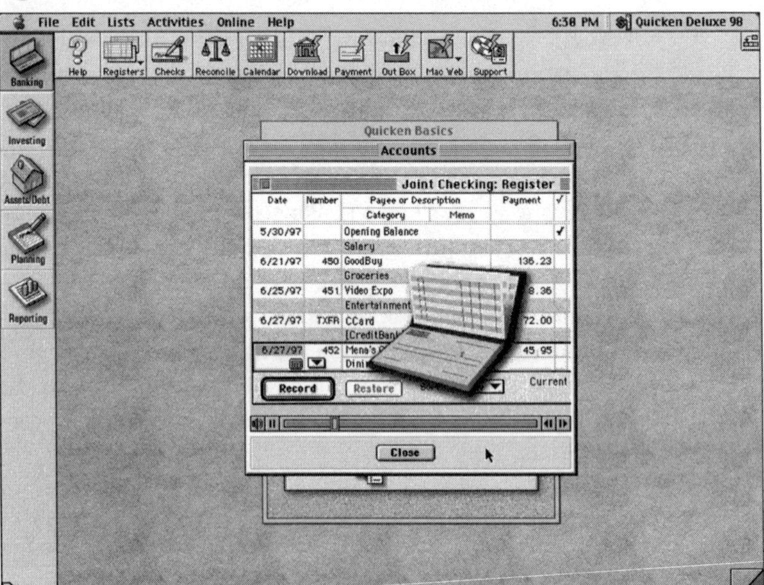

Mastering Everyday Skills

Putting aside the headache of an occasional glitch and the excitement of a flashy game, your iMac really shines at performing simple, everyday tasks. By that, I mean anything from checking the time and date to playing music. I haven't had the opportunity to cover all of these, nor can I in a book of this size, but I would be amiss if I didn't mention my favorites. So here are my top four everyday things the iMac can do.

Check the time and date

Your iMac displays the time in the upper-right corner of your screen. Click the time to see the date. You can modify your clock with the Date & Time control panel, too!

Save a text or graphic clipping

Choose Scrapbook from the Apple menu and paste in something you'd like to save. Now you can return anytime, locate your clipping, copy it, and paste it somewhere else. I use my Scrapbook all the time!

Remind yourself

Don't put a sticky note on your iMac itself; put it on your computer desktop! Choose Stickies from the Apple menu.

Listen to music

Pop an audio CD into your CD-ROM tray! If the sound is too low or high, adjust the volume on your Control Strip. Or choose AppleCD Audio Player from the Apple menu for more control (see Figure 11-5).

Figure 11-5: The AppleCD Audio Player works like a traditional CD player!

CLIFFSNOTES REVIEW

Use this CliffsNotes Review to practice what you've learned in this book and to build your confidence in doing the job right the first time. After you work through the review questions and the problem-solving exercises, you're well on your way to achieving your goal of using your first iMac.

Q&A

1. Which disk drive is built into the iMac?

a. 3½ floppy

b. CD-ROM

c. Zip

d. LS120

2. Which accessory is used to find files?

a. Nero

b. Sherlock

c. Francis

d. Kojak

3. Which of the following techniques enable you to select text?

a. Dragging the mouse pointer through the text

b. Holding down the Shift key while pressing cursor-positioning keys

c. Double-clicking a word

d. All of the above

4. Which type of graphic image is *not* supported by Web browsers?

a. CompuServe Graphics Interchange Format

b. Adobe Photoshop format

c. Joint Photographic Experts Group format

5. How can you get Balloon Help for an object on the screen?

a. Double-click it
b. Click it once
c. Point at it without clicking
d. Select it

6. Which printer connection works with the iMac?
   a. Serial
   b. Parallel
   c. USB
   d. SVGA

7. Which of these methods isn't recommended to shut down your iMac?
   a. Press the power button on the keyboard.
   b. Choose Special⇨Shut down.
   c. Press the power button on the iMac.
   d. Switch off the external power strip.

8. Which of these methods won't start an application?
   a. Double-click a document icon
   b. Choose Start⇨Run, then type the name of the application
   c. Drag a document icon onto its application icon
   d. Double-click an application icon

9. Which of these devices can provide pictures?
   a. Scanner
   b. Digital camera
   c. CD-ROM
   d. All of the above

10. Which application is used to write a letter?
    a. AppleWorks
    b. Internet Explorer
    c. Netscape Navigator
    d. Extension Manager

Answers: (1) b. (2) b. (3) d. (4) b. (5) c. (6) c. (7) d. (8) b. (9) d. (10) a.

Scenarios

1. You want to draw a picture of a golf course in AppleWorks. How can you make your sand trap look sandy?

 ____

 ____

2. You want to delete some text from an e-mail message. Explain how you can select text and delete it.

 ____

 ____

Answers: (1) First, select the sand trap outline in your drawing. Next, choose a sandy color from the palette at the bottom of the screen. (2) Point at one end of the text you want to delete, hold down the mouse button, and drag the pointer to the other end of the text. Release the mouse button, and then press the Delete key.

Consider This

- You have lots of ways to personalize your iMac to make it easier to use. For example, you can pick your favorite typeface and make it appear by default in AppleWorks. Check Chapter 6 for more.
- If you're faxing your resume to a prospective employer, don't print it on paper and run it through a separate fax machine. It comes out sharper if you fax it straight from the iMac. Look at Chapter 8 for the ins and outs of faxing.

CLIFFSNOTES RESOURCE CENTER

The learning doesn't need to stop here. CliffsNotes Resource Center shows you the best of the best — links to the best information in print and online about the iMac. Look for all the terrific resources at your favorite bookstore or local library and on the Internet. When you're online, make your first stop `www.cliffsnotes.com`, where you'll find more incredibly useful information about the iMac.

Books

This CliffsNotes book is one of many great books for your iMac from IDG Books Worldwide, Inc. So if you want some great next-step books, check out some of these other publications:

iMac For Dummies, by David Pogue, is your next logical step in learning all about your iMac. IDG Books Worldwide, Inc., $19.99.

Macworld Mac OS 8.5 Bible, by Lon Poole, shows how to use powerful tools and features that are built into the operating system of your iMac. IDG Books Worldwide, Inc., $39.99.

The Internet For Macs For Dummies, by Charles Seiter, is the ultimate iMac book for using the Internet. IDG Books Worldwide, Inc., $19.99.

You can easily find books published by IDG Books Worldwide, Inc., in your favorite bookstores, at the library, on the Internet, and at a store near you. We also have three Web sites that you can use to read about all the books we publish:

www.cliffsnotes.com

www.dummies.com

www.idgbooks.com

Internet

Check out these resources for more information on your iMac.

Apple's iMac Products Page, www.apple.com/imac, is the official home of the iMac.

Macintosh Discussion Groups, comp.sys.mac, is the home of Usenet discussion groups that cover of life with a Macintosh.

Next time you're on the Internet, don't forget to drop by www.cliffsnotes.com. We created an online Resource Center that you can use today, tomorrow, and beyond.

Send Us Your Favorite Tips

In your quest for learning, have you ever experienced that sublime moment when you figure out a trick that saves time or trouble? Perhaps you realized you were taking ten steps to accomplish something that could have taken two. Or you found a little-known workaround that gets great results. If you've discovered a useful tip that helped you use your iMac more effectively and you'd like to share it, the CliffsNotes staff would love to hear from you. Go to our Web site at www.cliffsnotes.com and click the Talk to Us button. If we select your tip, we may publish it as part of CliffsNotes Daily, our exciting, free e-mail newsletter. To find out more or to subscribe to a newsletter, go to www.cliffsnotes.com on the Web.

INDEX

G

H

I

J

K

L

M

N

O

P

COMING SOON FROM CLIFFSNOTES

COMING SOON FROM CLIFFSNOTES

Buying and Selling on eBay

Have you ever experienced the thrill of finding an incredible bargain at a specialty store or been amazed at what people are willing to pay for things that you might toss in the garbage? If so, then you'll want to learn about eBay — the hottest auction site on the Internet. And CliffsNotes *Buying and Selling on eBay* is the shortest distance to eBay proficiency. You'll learn how to:

- Find what you're looking for, from antique toys to classic cars
- Watch the auctions strategically and place bids at the right time
- Sell items online at the eBay site
- Make the items you sell attractive to prospective bidders
- Protect yourself from fraud

Here's an example of how the step-by-step CliffsNotes learning process simplifies placing a bid at eBay:

1. Scroll to the Web page form that is located at the bottom of the page on which the auction item itself is presented.
2. Enter your registered eBay username and password and enter the amount you want to bid. A Web page appears that lets you review your bid before you actually submit it to eBay. After you're satisfied with your bid, click the Place Bid button.
3. Click the Back button on your browser until you return to the auction listing page. Then choose View⇨Reload (Netscape Navigator) or View⇨Refresh (Microsoft Internet Explorer) to reload the Web page information. Your new high bid appears on the Web page, and your name appears as the high bidder.